Scarecrow

Social Fictions Series

VOLUME 45

The titles published in this series are listed at *brill.com/soci*

Scarecrow

By

J.E. Sumerau

BRILL

LEIDEN | BOSTON

All chapters in this book have undergone peer review.

The Library of Congress Cataloging-in-Publication Data is available online at
http://catalog.loc.gov

ISSN 2542-8799
ISBN 978-90-04-46814-6 (paperback)
ISBN 978-90-04-46815-3 (hardback)
ISBN 978-90-04-46816-0 (e-book)

ADVANCE PRAISE FOR
SCARECROW

"Questions of identity, belonging, family history, and regional imprint permeate the pages of Sumerau's latest novel. *Scarecrow* brings together the strands of a life, told through the memories that give it meaning and form. Through evocative first person accounts that blur the lines between auto/ethnographic storytelling and narrative fiction, this work encourages us to think sociologically about the innermost workings of our personal lives. It requires us to see the structural and institutionalized threads that weave the world as we know it over decades of experiences. This book would be useful for students in courses related to sociology, American studies, gender studies, and cultural studies; and for anyone interested in exploring the contents of their own life course."
– Austin Johnson, Ph.D., Kenyon College

"In a fictional story about a working-class, white, queer person growing up in the Southern United States that is worthy of reading for pleasure alone, J.E. Sumerau provides us with a gothic novel that many social scientists will find valuable for courses in social psychology, family, gender, sexualities, race, life course, and more. *Scarecrow* encourages us to think about the complexity of how we become who we are through our interaction with others over time. It is a true sociological novel!"
– Kim Davies, Ph.D., Augusta University, author of *The Murder Book*

"In *Scarecrow*, Sumerau provides an eye-opening experience for readers and students, especially those unfamiliar with hardship; an experience that affords them a new lens to appreciate the diversity and difference in the world around them. Through the storytelling of the narrator, Erin, an adopted, queer, trans, white, and working-class person in the South, Sumerau adds to the limited fiction work that explores the lives of queer people in the South struggling to make

sense of ourselves and our worlds. *Scarecrow* is a novel that explores many issues of our humanity that some would prefer to remain hidden, but that are vital to understanding society and addressing social inequality."
– **Baker A. Rogers, Ph.D., Georgia Southern University, author of *Trans Men in the South: Becoming Men***

"Rarely do novels provide the clear sociological lens we need to connect an insightful read with deeper critical thinking. In walking through slivers of memories of their relationship, education, and work trajectories, Erin, the narrator of *Scarecrow* by JE Sumerau, does just that. Taken together, Erin's life stories present a narrative perfect for use in gender, sexuality, inequalities, family, or social psychology courses, as the ambiguity we feel surrounding our identities, where we came from, and who plays a part in our lives resonates with their experiences. Their perspectives on race and death scattered throughout the text also provide relatable snapshots of how these factors frame the life course of working class, white Southerners."
– **Summer Roberts, Ph.D., University of South Carolina Beaufort**

"From the start of *Scarecrow*, Sumerau grabs readers by the hand and leads them on an endless, breathtaking journey of heart, hope, and all the emotions we are capable of manifesting. Whether reading about individuals like Erin for the first time or experiencing a personal sense of déjà vu in her narrative, you become deeply invested in Erin's journey. Sumerau's writing style cuts deep, making you laugh and cry in the same sentence; leaving readers shocked when they realize how much time has passed while being part of Erin's life. As with all of Sumerau's novels, I find myself drawn back in over and over, discovering new joys and cheering alongside Erin, crying and yelling into the pages, and – ultimately – recommending its heartfelt and important messages about life, love, and sense of identity to all readers."
– **Lacey J. Ritter, Ph.D., Wingate University, author of *Sexual Deviance in Health and Aging***

"Sociology courses inevitably lead us, as instructors, to help students connect their personal experiences to the increasing mass of demographic data we are flooded with on a near-constant basis. This connection with personal experiences helps students relate to the experiences of others. Of all the courses I teach, connecting students to the abstract, and the other is often the most difficult part of my Sociology of the South course. This is because the region is so unique in so many ways, yet often described as quintessentially more 'American' than the rest of the United States. In a way that neither the sociologist nor the artist in me can fully explain, the literary story combined with the social scientific approach of *Scarecrow* in, and of the south, enables both students and the casual reader a way to assess and understand their own, and others' experiences regardless of where they are from, where they are or where they are going."
– **Jason Eastman, Ph.D., Coastal Carolina University**

"*Scarecrow* is a fresh, intoxicating read you will not want to put down. Following the story of Erica, a bisexual nonbinary trans feminine person, the reader learns what has made her uniquely complex: her pain and joy. *Scarecrow* tells an important – and often ignored – story of a queer southerner. Sumerau weaves together social psychological concepts of identity development without losing the fascinating narrative. The novel *Scarecrow* would be a great addition to an academic course on social psychology, sexualities, the South, and gender studies."
– **M.C. Whitlock, Ph.D., University of North Georgia**

"*Scarecrow* is a beautifully written novel that captures the complexities of navigating life's traumas and what it means to be human. Sumerau weaves together a series of reflections throughout the narrator's life in a non-linear fashion – much like the stages of grief or processing trauma, love loss, or our own gender and sexual identities are not linear. *Scarecrow* reminds readers that our bodies, both mentally and physically, are imprinted by these life events and sometimes we end up forming decoy personas to protect ourselves in different spaces. More than ever, individuals need to see themselves reflected in a

contemporary novel like this to know they are not alone. *Scarecrow* would make a great addition to undergraduate courses addressing trauma, body and embodiment, mental health, sexualities, gender identities, families, aging, or human development."
– **M.N. Barringer, Ph.D., University of North Florida**

Previous Novels by J.E. Sumerau

Cigarettes & Wine

Homecoming Queens

Other People's Oysters
(with Alexandra C.H. Nowakowski)

Palmetto Rose

Via Chicago

For Shay

CONTENTS

CONTENTS

PREFACE

Who am I?
Where did I come from?

These questions permeate the pages of *Scarecrow* wherein a bisexual, nonbinary trans feminine person named Erin seeks to make sense of her life in relation to the places, people, and events she has seen and left behind over time. As the novel begins, Erin tells us that "39 funerals, 35 years, and too many lovers to bother remembering brought me to this point." From this opening statement, Erin reflects on three-and-a-half decades of experiences growing up working class, white, and queer in the southeastern U.S.; navigating sexual, gender, classed, racial, and religious meanings and relationships; surviving varied types of love, trauma, kindness, and violence; and joining the upper-middle class world of the professoriate. As the novel progresses, she shows us how these experiences intertwine, create opportunities, and leave scars that together fashion who she has become over time and in relation to others.

What are the contents of a life course?
What fractions of our lives do we use to narrate the whole?

Told through a series of vignettes reminiscent of diary entries or transcripts from counseling sessions, *Scarecrow* explores the construction of biography and identity as well as transformations that impact such efforts over the life course. As Erin's current and past experiences unfold over four decades, she seeks to integrate traumatic and joyful experiences into a cohesive sense of self and a biographical rendering of her experience. *Scarecrow* is thus a novel about the many ways we all seek to integrate varied notions of who we are, who we want to be, and who we think we used to be into ongoing experiences, events, and relationships throughout our lives. Built via non-linear reflections, *Scarecrow* illustrates the work we all do to fashion our identities over time.

How did I get here?
Where am I going?

I began writing *Scarecrow* as the same type of narrative reflection I have had people do and been asked to do myself in counseling sessions. It was initially an attempt to make sense of the transformations in my own life, rather than a planned attempt to construct a new novel. Somewhere in the process, I began to interweave stories from interviews I had done with many other people, and in so doing, Erin, as a character and a life course, emerged as a mixture of lived experiences narrated by people across the south. As someone who has done academic work, counseling, teaching, and advocacy related to trauma recovery and identity construction, I sought to capture the complexity of such experiences as well as the ways these experiences impact the life course. I further sought to highlight the experience of seeking to integrate disparate lives. Although Erin is ultimately a fictional character, her life course demonstrates the complexity and confusion of what it means to develop selves in relation to broader social, psychological, and physical norms and contexts.

Why am I here?
What does it all mean?

As such, I close this preface with questions readers might consider while following Erin's life course. Since this novel could be utilized in the teaching of sociology, social psychology, Symbolic Interactionism, narrative, families, gender, sexualities, race, class, geography, biography, Southern Studies, LGBTQIA studies, trauma recovery, or courses about aging and the life course, I would ask readers to think about how the people and places we encounter shape who we believe ourselves to be; what role the past plays in who we are and how we see ourselves and others; and when looking at ourselves today, how did we get here. *Scarecrow* can, of course, also be read entirely for pleasure, but even in such cases, I would suggest readers consider who they are and how they got here.

ACKNOWLEDGMENTS

Thank you to Patricia Leavy, John Bennett, Jolanda Karada, Henriët Graafland, and everyone else at Brill and the *Social Fictions* series for your faith in me, your willingness to support creativity, and your invaluable guidance. I would also like to especially thank Shalen Lowell for your considerable assistance and support. I cannot overstate how much the efforts and support of all you means to me. Thank you to everyone at Brill for supporting this book and my growth as an author.

Thank you especially to my spouse Xan Nowakowski for giving me the courage to write novels in the first place and walking by my side as I completed them and sent them out for consideration. My books would not exist without your inspiration, guidance, and faith, and I will never be able to thank you enough for what your support and encouragement means to me.

I would also like to thank Lain Mathers, Nik Lampe, Eve Haydt, Shay Phillips, and Brittany Harder for providing constructive comments and insights throughout this process and my life in general. There is no way for me to express how important each of you are to everything good about my life and writing.

I would also like to thank some people I have only met once in passing after a concert. This work was written while I listened nonstop to the Counting Crows, and their records provided the soundtrack for the writing, editing, and revision of the work.

Finally, this novel would not be possible without the years of research I have done on sexualities, gender, religion, violence, and health. I have had the privilege of interviewing and observing so many wonderful southern LGBTQIA people over the years, and many of their experiences find voice in this novel. I would thus like to thank all of them for sharing their stories with me.

CHAPTER 1

39 funerals, 35 years, and too many lovers to bother remembering brought me to this point.

***

The first thing I ever told my father was a lie. Okay, he wasn't really my father at the time, but more like the person who donated the sperm that allowed me to exist. And okay, it wasn't the first thing I said to him because from what I can gather, I could say a word or two before he gave me away when I was about two years old. And okay, it wasn't exactly that I told a lie by saying something false, but more a lie of omission if we want to get technical, and I've heard many people say that those don't necessarily count as lies or count as much as explicit lying. This, of course, is my problem, as my oldest friend would say, I can frame and reframe any set of details to tell anywhere from one to a million versions of the same story.

In any case, the first time my sperm donor and/or biological father and I stood somewhere together I was being dishonest. We were on a sidewalk on the Upper West Side of Manhattan. He was in his forties. I was in my twenties. He was working for a non-profit of some sort. I was in college and working at a hotel that would have to be renovated to be a piece of shit. It was the first time we had seen each other – that we knew of, I guess – since I was just about two years old. It was only a couple months since I got an email from him at work one night after he learned I was looking for him. Or, that's why he said he wrote, but his sister knew I was looking for him since the mid-nineties, so I always thought maybe he started things out with a lie too. It didn't really matter to me at the time, and I don't know if it does now.

I would like to say that the lie came from a good place, but that would only be half the story. The good place was the part of me that wanted him to have the good feeling he seemed so desperate for at the time. It seemed incredibly important to him, for some reason I could not guess, to give me or show me something new. Maybe it was

1

because he discarded me like trash when I was younger, or maybe it was because he had some insecurity issues. Or maybe it was something else entirely, I don't know, but it seemed like it mattered to him a lot. I could say that I told the lie so he could have this. In this version of what happened, he asked me if I was "excited about seeing New York for the first time," and I let him believe it was my first time in New York. Hell, maybe I did explicitly lie and say it was, I don't remember. In this version, I went along with his desire to show me the city so he could feel good about giving me something after two-plus decades of giving me absolutely nothing. I like this version.

Of course, there is at least one more version of this story. Though I don't like to think about it, the fact is that I wanted to know him, at least for a little while, and for some reason, I wanted him to give a damn about me. I still do. He still doesn't, except on occasion, best I can tell. In this case, it may be that I played along for the same reason I was on my best behavior from the moment I received his first email until about three years later – I wanted to know him and didn't want to scare him off. I mean, I already had evidence that he was good at running away from difficult things. In this version of the story, I played along so he would be happy enough to keep talking to me and kept up the act for the entire three years we were on speaking terms the first time around. Unfortunately, there is evidence for this version as well since it was only when I finally, after three years mind you, stood up to him in a disagreeable manner for the first time that I no longer heard from him – discarded like the same trash I was as a child again as an adult. In this version, however, it is not his feelings I am protecting, but rather, my own selfish desire for some semblance of a relationship with this fella I spent so many years wondering about.

I like to think it was the former, but the latter version is equally possible. In any case, I pretended I had never been to New York throughout my visits to see him in 2006 and 2007. I had been in the city for the first time in 2001, right before there were no longer twin towers, but I just left this part of my life out of the story. The fact was I had even been on the same street before because my adoptive mom had an address for him on that street that I searched for in 2004 before I realized that I was missing the apartment number. I remember wondering what it would have been like if we had passed in the street. Would I recognize him? Would we look alike or walk alike or talk alike? I stood there in my joy and dishonesty that day in 2006 realizing that the answer to all three questions was an emphatic yes. After a lifetime of not having anyone around who looked like me, it was a little creepy standing there in front of an older version of most of my own face. Sometimes when I think about this now, I wonder if maybe he lied too – maybe he saw me on the street in 2004, ran away, and didn't want to admit it. Maybe we were both living in a fantasy we each allowed the other to have.

***

My first exposure to the Catholic Church almost led me to convert. I wasn't actually there for the service. I wasn't actually there for the religion. I wasn't even there because my youth baseball team often practiced on the fields owned by the church in question. I was looking for Yvette in a momentary lapse of cowardice. I was hoping to see her. I was hoping she would see me and take something good from the observation. I was not planning to pay any attention to the service at all, but then the guy wearing a dress came out and suddenly I wanted to be Catholic. I loved wearing dresses when I could get away with it. I would borrow them from my sister's closet without permission when I was in the house alone, and desperately hope I could hear anyone arriving back home in time to get rid of them. If Catholic males could wear dresses, I wanted to be a Catholic.

I would, of course, learn years later that the guy was wearing something that looked like a dress to my young eyes, but was not considered a dress. I would learn that wearing a dress among Catholics when one didn't look like they were born with a vulva could be just as damnation worthy as doing so in the Southern Baptist Church I went to as a child. I would learn all these things later – and remember that I went there that day to talk to Yvette – but at the time, I spent the rest of the service watching the dress – uh, robes – and thinking about conversion. It wasn't that I was all that religious in the first place, at least not in a spiritual sense. Jesus and I agreed to disagree before I even reached a decade of age. No, that wasn't it. It was that I was raised in South Carolina where even the notion that you could live without going to churches was something it would take me years to realize. If I had to go to one anyway, I just thought it would make more sense to go to one where I could wear dresses *and* pants instead of having to pick a side. My inability to pick a side – in multiple domains – would become a central aspect of my life over time, but we'll get to that.

I also think I was drawn to religions at the time because the boys I kissed at the church were different than the girls I kissed outside of the church. Even though I was only thirteen when I saw the guy in the dress – uh, robes – I already noticed this difference. There was something, I like to call it fear until I think about how that might sound to other people, that the boys I kissed in the library of the church had that the girls did not. The girls were generally curious, funny, talkative, and smart. The boys were looking over their shoulders, shaking, and hesitant. I liked spending time with the girls more, but kissing the boys was more fun because it almost felt like its own secret adventure due to the ever-present sense of, well, fear. There was something exhilarating about that fear, my own as well, and the chance of being caught at any moment. I liked it. I didn't believe in the spiritual stuff even then, but I sure did believe in the power of fear to take an ordinary thing – like a kiss – and turn it into something dangerous and beautiful at the same time.

***

The first time I ever felt guilty involved a broken ass, a breakup, and a day I still cannot actually remember, but have pieced together from the accounts of others. I was in my early thirties, and for the first time since I was just into my twenties, I was in love. I don't mean the Hallmark card kind of shit. I mean the feel like you would dive in front of a bullet for another person kind of thing where it aches – just in different ways – whether you are around them or without them. I was emotionally stunted long before they found me trying unsuccessfully to seem like a human at a picnic with a bunch of people from our work, but I don't think I knew just how messed up I had become until I lost almost three months of conscious knowledge or memory about my own life a few weeks, best I can tell, after I realized that I would be severely damaged if they were not around anymore. The last time I felt like that I was severely damaged in the end.

This was the issue that led to – best I can tell from how others describe the emotion in books, movies, and Hallmark cards – my first experience with guilt. During the three months I was apparently a zombie without any ability to consolidate or access memory, we became closer to each other than was likely possible for my conscious self. As others have in similar blackouts or traumatic response episodes, I sought to destroy this connection before it could destroy me. This was not successful, I should note, but I tried, nonetheless. I accomplished this by – without any awareness or memory of the experience, mind you – shutting down physically and emotionally more and more over the course of a summer until I finally walked out on the greatest love of my life on a day where they had become injured and at a time where I had nowhere to go. Walking out on someone in pain, I am my birth father's child I used to say, was nothing new. Having nowhere to go was also something I was familiar with, and surprisingly or maybe just sadly, comfortable with. What shocked me was that I felt bad about it.

I don't mean that I felt bad in the way you say, "Awe shucks," when your day doesn't go right or when you start cursing because the fucking barista messed up your order or even when you get assaulted for no damn reason other than holding a cute boy's hand, I don't mean normal sadness, regret, or other "I feel bad" type stuff. No, I mean I felt bad in the sense that I thought I should shoot myself, but then decided that was too nice for me. I mean I felt bad in the sense that I spent hours and even days a month later curled up in a ball crying and wishing to just die already. I mean I felt bad in the sense that someone could have slowly and carefully carved all the skin off of my body while I was watching, and I would have felt like I got off easy. Best I can tell, I felt bad in the sense that I felt guilty. I did not like that feeling.

***

The first time I kissed a boy happened in the woods behind my house. Well, they weren't behind my house so much as diagonally across from the lot behind my house. They also stretched all the way to the other side of town. They ran behind my neighborhood, behind a park, behind another neighborhood, and finally under the bridge that left South Carolina for the only-a-little-bit more interesting city across the river. I can't say I really knew the boy all that well. We were on a baseball team together – ah Little League memories – but he lived in a different neighborhood where all the houses had two stories and multiple cars.

Even though I was only six years old, I remember the day like it was yesterday. He walked up to me after practice, and said, "I'm going to throw some sticks in the stream by the big black pipe, wanna come?" I went with him into the woods thinking nothing of it, and we made our way to this massive ravine on the side of what used to be railroad tracks and would one day become a walking path that hugged the river. My neighborhood was beyond the woods on the other side of those same tracks. Above the ravine and stretching across it, there was a big black, I guess water, pipe that every kid dared other kids to climb across. Some idiots even did it. We are probably lucky none of them dropped over 100 feet to their deaths in the process, but I don't recall ever thinking about that as a kid, even the time I went across it. In the bottom of the ravine, there was a small stream that wound from the river, through the ravine, underneath what used to be a railroad track, and into the woods on the other side.

When we got to the stream, the boy – whose name I want to say was Will, but I'm not sure – said, "You ever get curious about stuff."

"I am always curious about stuff all the time," I said. This was, and remains, very true.

"You ever get curious about kissing?"

"I don't know," I said, and this was true too. I kind of liked the sight of it on television, but I had not given the topic any thought yet. This was about to change.

"Sometimes I think it would be fun." I nodded, and simply waited to see what he would say next. "But I guess you have to practice to get good, and I wouldn't want some girl to think I was gross." This was solid six to eight – which was his age – year old logic, I thought. "I guess I just wish there was some way to practice or something."

I admit I was guessing here, but I guessed right so it worked out. I said, "We could practice." The fact that I had already beat this kid up once, I think, helped me say these words. In any case, I guessed right, and we practiced. We practiced about thirty-seven times over the next six weeks, in fact. It was nice. It was fun. It was, I somehow already knew though I can't recall the specific church service where I learned this, a cool way to make baby Jesus cry. It was also what led to the first time I kissed a girl almost six months to the day later.

CHAPTER 2

Sometimes people call me Edwin. Sometimes people call me Erin. Sometimes people call me other things. Some of these other things I like. Some of these other things I do not like. No matter what people call me, I still have no clue who I am.

***

The worst thing I ever told Nikki was the truth. We met at a going away party at a small pizza place in South Carolina. I was leaving for graduate school. She was dating a former roommate and current friend of mine. There was something about the red she was wearing that made me want to stay in South Carolina a little longer. There was something, she said, about my personality that was like nothing she had ever known before that night. We spent the night ignoring the friends of mine who were supposed to be saying goodbye to me and talking to each other about all kinds of things that had nothing to do with her date or my move.

This all seemed innocent enough until we met up by accident a couple months later when I was visiting my hometown, situated across the river from her hometown, and she was having coffee without anyone else. We spent another evening talking the night before I dumped my college girlfriend and college boyfriend as I had planned to do on that visit and for months before I left for graduate school. I wasn't all that interested in either one of them, but they were interesting enough to mess up beds with while I was busy with my undergraduate course load, my newfound conversations with my birth father, and my hotel job. I don't know what happened to either of them, but I do know that the college girlfriend's promise to commit suicide when I ended things with her in a mall parking lot turned out to be lies because I found out later she had a kid with someone I never met. Well, actually, Nikki found out about this and told me while we giggled on the bed we were sharing by then.

Nikki and I began trading messages on the internet and later fluids in hotel rooms when I visited the city in between our hometowns – the same city where she went to college, and where I graduated college the year before. My friends didn't know. Her friends didn't know. My old friend who she was still dating didn't even know yet, and he kind of had the right to know, all things considered. We got along especially well because she was bored out of her mind in that city just like I had been, and I was increasingly lonely and isolated surrounded by other graduate students who grew up with more money, who were almost entirely heterosexual and cisgender, and who all found graduate courses stressful. I'd had a gun in my face three times by this point in my late twenties, no class was going to stress me out. We talked about her boredom and my isolation, and we spent time together when I visited.

Well, that was what we did until the holidays at the end of my first semester of graduate school. I was thinking about not going back – it felt like I was stuck in some white middle class heterosexual cisgender club where numbers were magic and the realities of people who were not in the listed groups were yet to be discovered by folks with degrees and data sets. I wanted out. Nikki and I were in a cheap hotel, but not the one I worked at in college because my old friend who she was maybe living with kind of now worked there. She was considering going out west and saying, "Fuck college," because she was having trouble affording it and hating all the people there for varied reasons. Thinking about this, it hit me that if I had one other bi person from the working and lower class with me, graduate school might not be so bad. She was interested in getting out of town, and I was interested in not having to find a job, so I suggested she move south with me. She said she wanted to, but only if I needed her. I know that she meant "need" in more of a romantic or friendship or something way, but I ignored that, kept silent about my need for someone who could somewhat understand me, and told her, truthfully, mind you, that I needed her. That was it. We were moving. We were going to be a couple. We had to tell people who probably would not be very happy about this reality.

***

The last words I ever said to my grandmother were not nice. In fact, I told her I hated her, and stormed out of the house. She died not long after that.

Although I couldn't marshal the emotional maturity to feel guilty about it, this was especially unfortunate because my grandmother was one of the greatest features of my young life before that day. She had not only allowed me to dress as a woman at times when I visited her, but even made this possible by encouraging my visiting and making a wide variety of women's clothes available to me from the time I was about twelve. Some of my happiest and safest moments as a teenager came in the back room of her house trying on clothes – and personas – without having to worry about being caught, getting hurt, or anyone else knowing. I loved her more than most of the people I have ever known, and after learning about this guilt thing a couple years ago, I can't stop wondering if she ever knew that. I hope she did.

On the fateful day when we last spoke, I was nineteen. She was pushing one hundred. She was barely there mentally at that point, and I was used to the fact that she would mistake me for her long-dead son. It was three years after I found out she was actually my great-grandmother by blood, and that my birth father was actually her grandchild. She didn't know that I knew she was related to him. My adoptive parents didn't either. If his sister told him, then he knew, but I honestly don't know if she ever told him. It was actually the child of his other sister who told me. She wrote me a letter because she felt I had the right to know. No one else seemed concerned with me or my rights in that family at the time. She also thought, maybe she heard concerns raised about me at the time that were semi-correct, I should know that he was gay and gave me up so he could move north to live openly that way. As a bi and trans kid in South Carolina, I could empathize with him much more than I expected when I studied up on what small towns in East Texas were like at the end of the 1970's.

She was doing the – becoming – usual thing where she thought I was her son. She was talking to me about "that damn woman" who took me away to Louisiana and Texas. "That damn woman" was the mother of my birth father, and I called her by much worse names than that over the years since she never seemed to do anything but hate, lie to, and avoid me. This became tricky about a decade later when I learned that she was basically a hero to my birth father – as was the sister of his who never told me anything and even hid his existence from me with her own lies when I was a teenager. As I always did, I was enjoying this line of thought because other than the secret letters from my cousin, it was my only source of my biological roots. She was telling me about the importance of covering all my bases as I set up a trucking business – ironically enough, the decision to start that business would be the death of my birth grandfather and some say the reason I was abandoned or that my birth father finally felt free to run away up north. She knew all these details about trucking, and I remember wondering where she learned these things as a former mill worker in South Carolina.

I had gone into the back room to look at my collection of women's clothes for some reason I lost sight of after the events of the day. When I entered her living room, she was sitting in her favorite chair dipping her tobacco as she often did. She looked up at me, and said, "Well isn't this a surprise, I haven't seen you in so many years," before calling me by my birth father's name. I can't explain it even now, but I was glued to the spot. I thought my heart would explode. There were so many – way too many – feelings raging through my body for me to handle, and I just stared at her with eyes that I'm sure could kill in some science fiction movie made specifically for television. She started asking me questions about what I had been up to for the last couple decades, and then she said that name again. All I remember is that I told her I hated her and stormed out of the house almost – by the sound of it – breaking the door when I slammed it behind me. She was dead before we got a chance to talk again.

***

I stopped eating ice cream for over a decade. Before August of 1993, I really enjoyed the occasional scoop of ice cream. I would go with family, with friends, with dates or whatever you call boys and girls you want to kiss before you are a teenager, and with people from the church to this little ice cream shop with pink walls and mountains of stuffed animals on display. We would pick out our flavors, taste a few we knew we weren't getting because we could and laugh over a nice frozen treat. I stopped doing that after the last time I let my adoptive father take me out for ice cream.

I was twelve years old, going on thirteen as we said at the time, and he showed up in the backyard where I was building something for extra cash. I often built things when I was a kid. I found something magical about watching nothing become something. He showed up in the backyard and told me we should get some ice cream. I didn't ask any questions. I didn't argue. I didn't care where or why, I wanted ice cream. I would not feel that desire for over a decade after that day. I still don't know why he picked that day, or maybe why my parents picked it together is more accurate, I don't know that either. Twelve and a half seems an odd age for such a thing. A random day in August seems just as odd. I sometimes wonder if something happened that I still don't know about to force the issue. Maybe they were hearing things about my extracurricular – read bi and trans – activities. Maybe they were worried about me for some reason. Maybe it really was random. Maybe I should ask.

Whatever the reason, that day is crystal clear in my mind for two reasons. First, it was the first time in my life that my life made any damn sense. I had always been different than everyone I had ever met, and that day, I had at least one reason for it. I still have no clue how useful that reason actually is, but it made sense at the time. Second, it was the day in my life where I first experienced what psychiatrists and counselors would call a blackout. I always had an amazing memory, and I still do in many respects. On that day, however, most of my life before I was twelve disappeared. Things I wrote about in my little journal I kept hidden in my bedroom just disappeared. They had been full memories before that day, and suddenly, they were gone. I now understand that it was likely my brain dealing with overwhelming emotions – hell, I can even explain it scientifically in the latest peer-reviewed ways – but I'm still not sure how the hell it happened or why it bothered me so much for years to come.

Whatever the results, we went to get ice cream. We got to-go cups from the usual place I went with everyone else, and then we went to a park nearby. It wasn't the park near our house. It was another one that was on the other side of the church from where we lived my whole childhood. I don't know why we went there instead of somewhere I normally went, but that was what we did. We sat in a parking lot beside some tennis courts I would visit a lot in college. I had never played tennis, didn't do that until college, but I remember staring at the courts while he spoke. I also remember wanting him to shut up and keep talking at the same time. That didn't make sense to me then, any more than it does now, but I remember it. He explained, or said without much explanation actually, that I was not always their child. He said that my mom, "Went out to Texas to get you from some other people who couldn't take care of you." He said a lot of other things that day, but I just remember staring at my ice cream.

***

"Please don't fuck me, Ben," Martini says into Ben's crotch as Ben helps him stumble across the alley toward where I parked the car. Martini is not Martini's nickname yet. That will happen the next morning, but I have trouble calling him anything else these days. We are in college. Well, I am. Ben is taking a semester off even though he only has one semester left to graduate and even though the one semester off will turn into nine. Martini is considering applying to community college or technical college or whatever it is called but hasn't sent in the paperwork yet. I am twenty-six years old and so is Ben, but Martini is only twenty. Martini has just earned what will become his nickname by illegally drinking about thirteen martinis of varied types and varied mixed liquors at the bar we are leaving. It is his first time drunk. He is still trying to figure out if he is bi like Ben and me. Ben has a crush on him that he knows about. We've been hanging out for only three months, but it is the beginning of a long-term friendship.

The three of us met when Ben and I realized that my car would not make the four-hour drive to Charlotte, and Ben asked Martini to drive us for a free ticket to the concert happening there. Ben already had a crush on Martini, but I had never met him. We were desperate to go see a new band – well, new to us, they had been around a decade or so – Ben discovered. The band is named Wilco, and we will all become even bigger fans – especially Martini, as he had no knowledge of the band prior to concert – after the show. We will also get lost on the way, and bond over the experience. Martini will also tell us that he sometimes finds guys attractive, but that he struggles with this because he still believes in ghost stories – Christianity in this case – and the versions of those stories he has learned are not too fond of the gay or bi thing.

In the process of trying to figure out this tension between his Jesus and his desire for a Hispanic singer named Jesus performing at the bar that night, Martini gets drunk for the first time. We didn't bother to tell him ahead of time that mixing liquors is not the best idea. It was more fun to watch him learn that life lesson himself. It was equally fun to watch him outside on the bar's porch dancing with one of those metal heaters places sometimes put out in the winter. I don't tell Martini, but he also kisses the heater twice – each time pulling back with just a hint of pain in his eyes. Ben is helping him because he cannot walk on his own. To his credit, Ben does, in fact, not fuck him that night or ever.

CHAPTER 3

There was a field behind the empty lot across the street from the house I grew up in. In this field, there was a dirt road that made a circle. In my dreams, I visit this field a lot.

***

Yvette scared the shit out of me from the moment we met. This was not her fault. This is also something that I seriously doubt she knows. I never told her.

It was the first day of seventh grade, and I was sitting in the back of the classroom as I always did. It was easier to ignore the teacher and read whatever I wanted to read back there. Yvette came in, sat down in front of me, turned around, and started a conversation. This was not the scary part. She was obsessed with all kinds of silly things like cartoons, random questions about books, and for some reason, the idea of electronic pets that would, again for some reason, become very popular a few years later. This was not the scary part. She was maybe the strangest person I had ever met, and she owned it. She didn't want to fit in, best I could tell, but rather, she was alive in a way most people were too busy trying to fit in to ever be. This was not the scary part either. The scary part was that I didn't think I could lie to her.

I lied to everyone at the time. No one knew me, and I was happy about that. I don't know when I figured out you didn't tell people that you were bi or liked to dress like a girl, but I was well aware of this rule by the time I was in middle school. I don't know how I knew that people were often not as nice to adopted kids, but I somehow already knew. I don't know how I knew that it would be a bad idea if anyone found out I was dating and in love with a beautiful boy that went to another school, but again, somehow, I knew these things. My boyfriend knew these things too, and we talked about them between the two of us. We used coded notes and only met in the woods just in case we were right about this. We figured out in high school that we were right, and regretted having to learn for sure, but we'll get to that.

Yvette was the first girl I really liked, and I mean really, just like my boyfriend was the first boy I had serious feelings for. Whether the two things were connected or not, they were also the first two people I ever met that I was sure I would not be able to control what I said when they were around. This, right here, was what was scary about Yvette.

A couple years ago, I found Yvette on social media, and from what I can tell, she might have been a safe person to talk to about all the shit I was going through, but I did not know that then. Then, she was a breathtaking mind with a body that made me nervous. She was very talkative, and I wondered if talkative people could be quiet about some things. She was from one of the richest neighborhoods in town, which made me automatically have difficulty trusting her in the first place. I think about it now, and wonder if she might have been something special, but instead, she remains the – to use a phrase from too many bad movies – one that got away. I will never know what might have happened because the first thing I did when she asked me out – which in middle school is a weird question to begin with even if you don't have a secret boyfriend – was say yes because I couldn't stop myself, break up with her the next day because I was terrified I would answer any question she asked honestly, and start "dating" her best friend within the week because I hoped that would make her not like me anymore.

**

Amy said, "Thank you," as I finished putting my clothes back on, and placed a crisp, one-hundred-dollar bill on the bedside table. It wasn't the first time we slept together. It wasn't the first time I used one of the cheap dirty rooms at the hotel where I worked. It was, however, the first time I paid Amy like her normal customers did. I guess, theoretically, I paid her at other times by letting her use rooms for free or sharing my dinner with her, but this was the first time I ever gave her any cash. I only did it because her daughter was on the verge of no longer having daycare due to a slow week at the hotel.

Amy was an honor student at a private high school when we met in the 1990's, but by the time we saw each other again my first week working at the hotel in late 2005, she was not the same person. As she put it, the combination of drugs, unplanned pregnancy, and parents who found such things unsavory landed her on the streets. The streets, after a few months, landed her in an occupation that revolved around the number of truckers, road workers, and bored cops at the hotel in a given week. She was one of the four regular professionals that worked the hotel I worked at to afford my college education, but she was, by far, the most interesting one to me. She gained a reputation for pegging bored husbands in Christian, heterosexual marriages, and was especially talented with the strap-ons when the rich people came in each year for the Master's golf tournament that turned the 30-dollars-per-night rooms at the hotel into fought-over-almost-200-dollar-per-night rooms for about a week.

Her daughter was in an amazing pre-school-mixed-with-daycare program in the rich part of the city where the population was mostly white and did their best to ignore that other parts of the city did not have access to running water. It was the American dream, she would say, leave home early, grab some guy's boot straps while fucking him in the ass, and raise a child while running your own business and being your own boss. It amazed me that she was still a Republican. Her daughter's sperm donor was in college somewhere "up north," but she had not seen him since his family's lawyer threatened her a few months before the daughter was born. She said it was his lost. I didn't care. She thought I was nice. I didn't care.

Mostly for something to do in the middle of the night, I got in the habit of getting to know and sharing stories with the professionals – and some of their regular customers – my first year working at the hotel. The job was perfect for a college student since I had hours-upon-hours of nothing to do, and that made sure all the homework got done. It was also somewhat fascinating to listen to Lindsey talk about the names the truckers wanted to be called in bed, or to listen to Gary, the only male professional during my tenure at the hotel, talk about the ways the mostly women he saw avoided talking about anything at all. Gary was also a male model in a committed relationship with another man who always reminded me of Dewey from *Malcom in the Middle*, and he always said he was "only doing this until that big break." I think he even believed it each time he said it, but I never bothered to ask any questions.

***

I didn't really begin to understand racism until my friends and I played basketball at school the first time. We were starting first grade, and there was a sparkling, new asphalt court set up just down the hill from our classrooms. We didn't really care for the school part, but access to that basketball court was enough to get us to school early every morning and keep us there long after classes were finished. Before then, we played on a much less nice stretch of asphalt between the mostly black neighborhood on one side of the park and the mostly white neighborhood on the other side of the park. The problem, I guess, was that we never stopped to think that playing basketball at school would not be the same as playing it at the other court.

It probably never crossed our minds because the rules we already knew about were all the same on both courts. We were running back and forth, yelling at each other for no apparent reason, and enjoying the game. As was usual after years of practice by that point, everyone on the court was an N word. Everyone called at least most of the others this word, and everyone was called this word by most of the others. It was normal and had been during our games for as long as they had taken place. Well, it was normal until Lionel and I made the mistake of calling each other this word at about the same time in front of a passing teacher. She screamed at us and made us come with her to the principal's office. We would have to explain what the hell happened to the rest of the group after the fact. We were both berated by the principal next, though he never said why, and then sent home for the day.

When I got home, my parents were surprised. I showed them the note, and they yelled at me too. I asked them what was happening, and they said, I remember this word-for-word even though I was only seven at the time, "You don't say that word in public." This confused me because my dad said it all the time, about damn near everything, and all over the place. I asked why I should not say it in public and noted that he said it all the time. He said, "It's different nowadays, you're not supposed to talk about that kind of stuff no more because of the liberals." I didn't understand. That night, I met up with Lionel at the basketball court between the neighborhoods like we often did, and he said, "My dad said that word is evil, did you know that?"

"I had no clue."

"He said it's a way to say people like me are not as good."

"That makes no sense."

"That's what I said, and then I asked why he says it all the time if it's so bad."

"I asked the same thing."

"He said that's different because it's okay for us to say it."

"My dad said it's different because we're supposed to not say it in public."

"I don't get it."

"I don't either."

"Do you think I'm not as good as you."

"No, I mean, hell, you're better than me at math and basketball so how could you be not as good as me."

"Dad says white people think we're bad because of our skin."

"I don't understand." I really didn't understand, but after that day, I began to get an idea. We talked to his dad and grandma and mom, and they told us about things called segregation, lynching, slavery, and all this other stuff. I talked to my oldest sister, and she told me all kinds of terrible things that were still done to people just because they looked like my friend. She said that word is a symbol of something she called racism, and I should never use it again, even in private. I agreed with her. I didn't want to say my friend was lesser even accidentally. I asked her why no one taught me this stuff and why dad used the word. She said it was because of something called white supremacy and hatred, and that a lot of people, like dad, still saw people as less, but didn't want anyone to know because it was not polite anymore. I asked her how people ever believed that kind of stuff, but she didn't have an answer.

CHAPTER 3

***

Twenty years after I first started to learn about racism, a felt a bottle slam into my back and heard someone scream n-word-lover from a truck. I was walking with a guy I dated in college after having a nice meal together. We were talking about his plans to go to a school called Howard after graduation because he wanted to get a master's degree. It was our third date, and the nineteenth time – well, to that point – I'd been called an n-word-lover by a coward passing by since my first interracial relationship in the mid-1990's.

Especially at a time when a person of color was running for president and looked like he might even win, it was yet another reminder that no matter how much things change – or at least appear to change – they can also stay the same at the same time. My date was a total gentleman as he helped me remove my, now soaking wet, polo shirt. I was annoyed. He was even more annoyed. Our carefree date was over, it shifted into a political discussion about racism in the country, and things we could do about it, with each other, and more broadly. After years of studying the subject and a few dozen books I'd read, I was pleasantly surprised by how much more I could still learn. In the end, we had two more dates – both without racist cowards getting in the way – before he learned I was dating two other people and decided he wanted someone who would be monogamous and plan a future.

CHAPTER 4

A few years ago, I flew into the city my best friend lives in only to realize that upon my arrival they had left town. I feel like this says something about my life.

***

I was fifteen when I went to the first important funeral of my life. I know this may sound odd to people who have experienced little death in their lives, but after you get to a certain number of funerals – maybe twenty-two, I'm not sure – you start to sort them out in your head in terms of importance, or at least I did. In any case, some of them matter more than others. The one where it is your own child who died in the four-wheeler accident or your lover who was caught by a stray bullet in the accidental shooting "incident," for example, matter more to people than the one where your aunt you barely spoke to fell asleep with her pills and never woke up again. That's all I'm saying here – some matter more than others.

The first one that mattered to me was in 1996. It wasn't my first funeral, it was actually number four for those keeping score at home, but it was the first one that mattered to me because I was deeply in love with the guy who died. My on-again, off-again, first boy love, boyfriend throughout my pre-teen, teen, and early-twenties, let's call him Gillingham, I think he would like that, anyhow, my boyfriend and I were on a break when I met, let's call this one Dave, about nine months before Dave was the guest of honor at his own funeral. Dave was new to the area, and I originally started hanging out with him because I thought it would make Gillingham even more jealous than he was over my, then-current, girlfriend. Put simply, I thought maybe it would bring him back to my side. This was correct, though that didn't happen until Dave had already gone on to meet baby Jesus in the sky or Aruba or wherever such things happen since the storybook doesn't actually give an answer.

I don't know if Dave was interested in me, or temporary boys or people who were both boyish and also girls like I was or girls of any kind or anything for that matter, but he was a lot of fun to be around, and he had the cutest dimples that made me want to stare at him when he laughed. I do know, and I did before he died though I don't know if telling someone would have made any difference, that he was struggling with serious depression and self-medicating with whatever drugs he could find. He was already seventeen even though we were in the same grade, and his mom had a friend that would give him some prescription pills for a good roll in the hay. I remember he said it wasn't prostitution because it didn't involve money. A decade later working at the hotel, I would seriously doubt this type of definitional work, but it sounded fine to teenage me.

I was not prepared, however, for just how much it hurt when a friend of ours stopped by in the way-too-early-morning hours one Saturday to tell me Dave was dead. The friend in question was often our source for weed, alcohol, and drunken escapades in his father's Porsche at the time, but I don't remember a whole lot more about him. In any case, Dave had gone out to stay with his dad because he was having trouble in school – read getting into fights and failing classes while high on the drugs he got from his mother's friend. While out there, in the middle of the woods where even a Waffle House or a gas station would be a long drive, he became so desperate for a fix that he decided to try out this thing called huffing gasoline. At the time, there were other people doing the same thing, and we'd even heard a teacher talk about it in class. Sometimes when people did it, they got very high. When Dave did it, his heart died.

***

I was walking in the field behind the vacant lot near my house when I heard Kimber scream for the first time. I was surprised by the sound. She was surprised by the dead carcass of a pig turned inside out and left in the grass just outside the dirt road circle and just before the woods began. I couldn't resist knowing what the scream was about, so I saw it too.

The field was right below the parking lot of the community pool in the neighborhood. It had a dirt road that started at the parking lot and then made a horseshoe of sorts around rows of vegetables people who rented each row – or a few – planted. Outside the horseshoe, there was just barren emptiness with patches of grass here and there before the woods, for only about twenty feet, and then the track that used to be a railroad line. Kimber was eight and I was five when I started poking the pig carcass with a stick. For some reason, this made her scream again. There were rumors that teenagers did crazy, deviant things in the woods and in the field. I remember wondering if this was what the adults were talking about. It was not. I learned that later when I was a crazy, deviant teenager in the woods and in the field.

I mainly hung out with Kimber because she was always teaching me things, and because she thought it was funny when I wore her panties. Being funny, I thought, was a small price to pay for being able to wear panties. I would come to her with some new word I learned – like hotboxin' or blowjob or pussy or swizzle stick or whatever – and she would sit me down on her back porch a block away from my house or take me out into the field for a walk. She would then explain the new word in the most graphic way possible – though I didn't realize that until years later – including but not limited to demonstrations of how the word was used in various contexts. I enjoyed these lessons almost as much as I liked wearing her panties. When we found the carcass, however, she had nothing at all to say on the matter.

***

"Did you take your big test yet," my mom asks for the, by my rough count, forty-sixth time in the past two years. It is 2012. I took the test in 2010. I wonder if I'll be answering the same question for the rest of my life. We are talking on the phone for about five minutes or so – this is about how long I can stand being on the phone with my adoptive parents – like we occasionally do since I left South Carolina for good at the end of my undergraduate studies.

The big test she is talking about is what graduate programs call a comprehensive exam. At my program, this meant we were given a list of readings – a couple hundred – that the faculty believed were especially important, and later put into a room without internet access to answer three essay questions about the topics in these readings. It was not a hard test for me, but it was for others. I took it the same weekend I met my birth mother for the first time, but we'll get to that. My mom always asks this question for reasons that make no sense to me. I think it is her way of trying to show interest in my work and life even though she has no clue what a Ph.D. does or what college is like. She was born into a lower-class family in the early 1950's, and high school was the only education level she completed other than training to cut hair. She doesn't understand my life, but I think the question about the "big test" is her attempt to show she cares.

I would not ever say that I'm close with my adoptive parents, but I would say that I appreciate them and the fact that thanks to them, I always had a home. I also honestly think they deeply care about at least one version of me. In their minds, best I can tell, I'm always some version of myself they had in their heads when they adopted me. I think they like this version of me, though I'm not sure I have ever met this version of me. I don't know if this is correct, but I feel like it is because I've mentioned many aspects of my life over the years that they either ignored or simply never brought up again or asked questions about. I know they pray for me because they think I am going to hell, and that suggests they, on some level, may remember or be aware of some aspects of me we don't talk about, but I remain uncertain as to what version of me exists in their heads as we talk on the phone for five minutes or so after I say, "Yes, I took my test," only to once again notice that they never ask how it went.

***

The worst thing Danielle ever did was believe in me. I don't know if this is true in the grander scheme of Danielle's life. There is a lot about her life that I don't know or care about. What I mean here is that in terms of my life, this was the worst thing she ever did. Don't get me wrong, it might have saved my life, but it hurt her more than I'm proud of at the time.

I met Danielle the way you tend to meet single mothers who pay the bills waiting tables and pass the time doing cocaine – by accident. I was going to this diner in Edgefield County South Carolina after having a bit of an emotional breakdown and quitting my own cocaine habit. I would show up there around ten o'clock at night, and spend hours reading and talking to the waitresses before going home to sleep. I didn't really have much of a home. I was back in my hometown mostly full time, and so I stayed with my parents or I slept in my truck. Some nights I slept with whatever woman, man, or non-binary person I could find because it was nice to have a different bed occasionally. This was around the time I started making the occasional Christian cry, but we'll get to that. I was in that part of my mid-twenties that was still kind of like my early twenties, and I had a lot of failure and not much else to show for it. Danielle was working at the diner and living with her mother.

We bonded over bummed cigarettes from one another and cocaine memories – as well as me cheating occasionally on my newfound sobriety with her current stash. I didn't like myself very much at the time, and my best friend at the time who I barely know nowadays had just dared me to go to college and try to make something of myself. As a result, I decided to try out a college student version of myself with Danielle. I wasn't planning to actually go to college, but that was beside the point. I told her I was a student at the school I would go to the following year and graduate from a few years later, and that's why I read so much. I came up with this whole backstory about my decision-making process and desire to be a lawyer who represented single moms like herself. It was bullshit, but she bought it for some reason. Maybe she wanted to believe that she would go to college someday – something she said, but as of 2015, she hasn't done yet in the decade since. Maybe she liked the idea of dating a college student who was, as she put it more than once, going places instead of bumming around. I don't know.

In any case, I was primarily living with her a few months later. I helped take care of the kid, washed some dishes, and stole money from the bottles of coins her mom kept in her bedroom. I left everyday around three in the afternoon for my afternoon classes, and

I basically went to a bar I liked, hit on and sometimes scored with other people, and read until about midnight or so when I would return to her mother's house. She kept making these elaborate plans about our future, and I kept ignoring them. It was, for me, a fun time, and a chance to try to figure out what life path I would screw up next. It was, for her, a fun time, and a chance to think about a future away from her mother and diners and poverty. I didn't know that then, but I found out the same night that I got home and learned that she found out I wasn't in college.

She was devastated. She was also very angry. She cried a lot. None of this surprised me. What surprised me was that I felt sad. I didn't understand why until a few hours after I left her mother's house that night with everything I owned at the time. It hit me when I was driving across town to where my adoptive parents lived – she believed in me. People had rarely believed in me, if ever that I knew of, and yet she did. She thought I was better than I was, but I was living like the piece of shit most of my life had taught me I was supposed to be. It was an odd realization that someone had finally had some faith in me, but by the time it happened, I had already become the useless human it seemed like most of my teachers, religious leaders, adoptive parents, and even more than a few lovers always thought I was. It was the first time since my first love died that I cried, and it was also the reason I went to college.

CHAPTER 5

Whatever you do, don't owe a cocaine dealer who uses the product he cuts out of the for-sale bags himself twenty dollars at a time when said dealer is having a bad night. This is what I learned from seeing an acquaintance shot in an alley as a teenager.

***

I am afraid of Connecticut. I know that sounds crazy but bear with me a moment. I've visited a lot of places in my thirty-five-year life, but Connecticut is the one I plan to avoid above others from here on out. Don't get me wrong, I'm not afraid of the weather in Connecticut even though I've heard that can be brutal in the winter. I'm not afraid of the rich people or Ivy League assholes that seem to be everywhere in that state. I'm not even afraid of having to admit that the annoying town from the *Gilmore Girls* is not real. No, I'm afraid of Connecticut because, for some reason I cannot begin to imagine, it seems to collect people I'm not sure if I would be okay with meeting again.

Part of my experience as, well, how did Nikki put it, oh yeah, a "Slutbucket" is that I'm kind of used to the idea that people I've seen naked might end up in random places I visit. This is not that big of a deal for me, but Connecticut is different. For some reason, and sadly thanks to the advancements of social media in my lifetime I know this useless information, Connecticut has managed to collect a dozen different one-night-stands of mine over the years. I sometimes imagine there is some kind of club where they compare versions of me over brie or wine or something. "Well, when I met them, they were in real estate," one says, and another says, "Well, I met them after they left their second wife and just needed to touch a man." I feel like if I went to that state, and took the wrong road, I might get called eleven different names – I used one of the names twice if you're keeping score at home – in the same shopping center.

I'm not sure how I would handle that, and this gets even more complicated because there are three other people in the damn state who know my legal and/or pre-adoptive and/or "favorite alias" names already. Incidentally, I don't go by these names otherwise, and thus, I would notice if they were used in a random moment. As such, these folks could royally fuck up the other scenario, though it is fun to imagine some of my castaways settling down and getting married to each other. One of the three people who, for lack of a better phrase, "knows me" in the state is still my friend, and while I love seeing him at academic conferences, I will never visit him in that state. The other two – Yvette and my birth father who we'll call Mitchell for the rest of this diary – are people that even though it might be nice to see them again, it would also be potentially awkward or dangerous to do so with a flock of former naked companions roaming around the state.

***

"I blame *Melrose Place*," Hannah says after wiping the liquid that left my body a few moments ago off my pants, her chin, and the couch. We are in the television room of the activities complex our church built just as we were becoming teenagers in the middle of the 1990's. There are people playing volleyball upstairs, but as we have done since our first night here for "youth fellowship activities," whatever that means, we were watching *Melrose Place* downstairs.

This is my first experience with fellatio. I will give it in the coming years. I will get it again in the coming years. I will thank *Melrose Place*, per Hannah's request, for realizing this was a thing to be experienced in the course of a life. I am thirteen. Hannah is fifteen. I have a girlfriend and a secret boyfriend. Hannah has a boyfriend. I'm in my last year of middle school. Hannah is in high school. I don't know if any of these details matter, but they felt like they did that night. We were watching an episode, and Hannah asked if I had ever heard of blowjobs. Channeling my inner Kimber, I said yes and told her what I had heard. She had given one for the first time earlier that week, or since last week's episode if you prefer, and found that she liked doing it a lot more than she would have suspected. She told me this. I told her I had no data for comparison, though that was not how I phrased it at the time. She said I should. I said I would love to. She said how about now. I said okay. She waited for the commercial break.

***

One of the most interesting things I learned during my encounters with Mitchell in my late twenties was that we had a surprising similarity in our respective pasts. My birth father, who we're calling Mitchell now if you don't mind, was born in the 1960's and spent most of his early life in East Texas. This was not the similarity. He was a gay man then and still identifies as such now to the best of my knowledge. That was not the similarity either. He did dream of being a writer, which was a similarity, but it was not the one I found interesting. The one I found interesting involved truck stops.

When Mitchell was in his late teens in the 1970's, he would go to truck stops to fool around with men in their big rigs, in their normal-sized trucks, and in their cars. This was apparently a thing that happened, and that he learned about from others. As he explained it to me, the sex was fun, free, and easy. Nobody wanted to know each other, and nobody was going to out someone else for fear of it happening to them. He learned a lot about male-on-male sex, and what people liked. He learned a lot about what he liked. Other than a friendly weed, porn, and record shop where I might have been conceived, there were no "liberal" or "safe" places, and there were no bars for our people that he knew of in the area at the time. There is one now. I've been to it. I had a lot of fun that night, but that is beside the point. The point is that his experiences at truck stops were something we had in common, though I never told him that.

When I was a just-into-my-twenties grieving mess of cocaine and alcohol, I would go to truck stops in South Carolina to roam around the parking lots, smoke cigarettes, pick up my cocaine, and occasionally give or receive some head. It was at one of these truck stops that I met a long-haul driver named Marty that made regular trips up to New York and back down to Carolina. He had a wife and kid in Carolina, but he had a lot of use for a precocious young lover on these long drives. He also had great cocaine and a cute accent, so

I started going with him up the coast on his trips. We would ride up to New York, and then I would bum around the city, stay in fleabag motels or with people I slept with or with naïve college students I sometimes slept with and other times just robbed before they woke up in the morning, and a week or two later I would ride back south with him. I was his "paid-for-whore," as he put it, on the rides north and south, and it allowed me to keep a job at a gas station in Carolina while spending weekends and even weeks in New York, New Jersey, and even in Philadelphia one time. It was especially interesting for me to realize that Mitchell played at truck stops after a trucker with a need for good head created the opportunity for me to first come to New York and later pretend I had never been there.

***

I had just turned seven when I kissed a girl for the first time. In fact, it was a birthday present. It also took place in the same ravine under the same big black pipe where I first kissed a boy.

Looking back, I'm not surprised Kimber was my first time with a girl. For one thing, Kimber was my first in a lot of ways and my primary source of information whenever I wanted to know something adults didn't tell us about. There were so many things adults did not tell us about where I grew up. At the same time, Kimber was also the only person who knew about my first time with a boy, and she thought it was cute. She also thought, as she put it three months before our kiss and three months after that kiss, "So unfair that someone else got you before I did." I didn't have any clue what was unfair about it, but I often had very little clue about the things other people seemed to care about. This is still the case.

We were on our way to the river. Kimber and I spent many afternoons sitting on the banks watching the water, and the occasional cottonmouth, in front of us. We were halfway across the ravine – in between the tracks that used to have trains and the river, standing beside the stream underneath the black pipe that stretched across the ravine parallel to both the river and the tracks – when she stopped walking for no reason I could determine at the time. "Is this where that mean little boy stole my first kiss," she said giggling.

"Yes, almost the exact spot."

"Where is the exact spot?"

I moved her over about a foot, and said, "There, why?"

"Because sometimes symmetry is important."

"Symmetry?"

She didn't respond. Instead, she took my face in her hands, and kissed me softly on the lips. She pulled back and asked what I thought. I thought it was nice. She told me later that some people only liked boys or girls, and she wanted to make sure I enjoyed the kiss before going for more of them. I did enjoy it. I told her so under the big black pipe on my birthday. She smiled and kissed me again. We didn't go to the river.

CHAPTER 6

You will know that you have fallen in love for real when someone shits and pukes all over your car, and not only do you clean it up without any annoyance, but you still want to fuck them at times when they are literally exploding with sickness.

***

The first time I fell in love did not involve an actual person. I don't know how normal or abnormal this is, but it is not something I ever see talked about all that much. Most of the time, people talk about the first boy, girl, or otherwise gendered being that swept them off their feet. I had these experiences too, but they weren't the first time I felt butterflies. At other times, people talk about this or that family memory, but my guess is I didn't have that kind of thing, that kind of connection to family, because I was left with little by way of emotional family memories after learning I was adopted. I feel like I would have kept the first love memory, but who knows. As such, the first time I felt like my chest swelled however many sizes too big did not involve interaction with a person, but rather, it involved the sound of a needle poking a piece of vinyl.

I think I was four years old, but I might have been five when the record player was moved into my bedroom, which was once my older-than-me-but-younger-than-my-other sister's room until my oldest sister moved out of the house. From what I've gathered, these movements occurred around the time I came to Carolina in the first place. In any case, the record player was moved into my bedroom for some reason to save some space somewhere. That same record player still lives – and works by the way – at the house today, but it lives in another room now. Tapes or cassettes were all the rage at the time, and we were a few years from people of our economic class even knowing what compact discs were in the mid-1980's. I remember getting new releases on cassette as late as the mid-1990's, but my first love was a format that was going out of style around the time I was emerging on the planet.

When the record player was moved into my room, my oldest sister gave me one piece of vinyl in a shiny dust jacket so I could see what the machine did. She was a fan of vinyl, and still had many of them at the house she shared with her husband and his soapbox racer collection. She showed me how to use the machine. She placed the record on the platter, set the needle, and adjusted the speakers. She left it playing when she left the room. She went out to do whatever older people did together during such visits at the time. I stayed in my room. I played the same side of the record 22 times because I didn't know yet to turn it over for more sounds. I sat on the floor listening to Elton John sing his *Greatest Hits – Volume 1* if you're interested – the rest of the afternoon. I was transfixed. I was in love. I was excited more than I would be about anything until I discovered a wide variety of physical sensations later in life.

Even now, three decades later, very few things please me as much as the sound of a record spinning on a turntable. Turntable is what I would learn to call the machine. I feel this way to an extent with other music on other formats, but there is a physical and emotional reaction to the sound of a needle dropping into a vinyl groove that transcends everything else I've seen on the planet, except for maybe intimacy, orgasms, and the sound a lover you truly love makes when they laugh unexpectedly as a result of something goofy you do. This obsessive kind of love manifested itself almost immediately with records, and never went away. When I say almost immediately, I'm not joking. A few hours later my oldest sister came back for her record, and I planted myself firmly wrapped around her legs crying and whining with all my might until she agreed to let me have the Elton John record. As a testament to just how cool she was about the whole thing, beyond that moment where I got to keep the Elton John record, I also only had to get caught stealing about six records from her before she started giving me records I could keep on a regular basis. After she died, I wondered if she ever knew that I actually got away with six more records during my brief stint as a music thief.

***

I was 33 years old when I saw a picture of me for the first time. I don't mean that there were not photographs of my physical appearance before I was 33. No, my family, like so many others, took photos of everything they could take photos of throughout my life. I knew what I looked like to others from these photos, but it never matched what I looked like in my head, on the inside, it never matched me. I found that match accidentally while digging through discounted CD's in a record store in Tallahassee, Florida in 2014.

I was doing something I had been doing my whole life – looking through records that were cheap to see what, if any, new things I might like to try out. When you want to hear everything ever released and spend most of your life listening to music, you learn to budget your music needs accordingly, the same way others do with necessities from what I can tell. Sometimes this means you only get budget bin albums for a little while because you have to pay your rent. Sometimes this means you get new releases even if that means you skip a meal or two because one of your favorite artists has a new album coming out. Sometimes this means you sleep with people specifically because you want to make copies of the CDs they keep in the little book – you know the kind, we all used to have them – in their car. You get the idea, you prioritize the things you cannot imagine living without, and for me, one of those is music.

I was continuing this lifelong ritual when I stopped unexpectedly. There, on the cover of an album I had never heard of by a singer I had never heard of, was a picture of the me that lived somewhere in my head, and that, despite lots of education related to makeup, prosthetics, and other tools, an image I had never gotten close to being able to match with my outside. I stood there staring at the album cover for long enough to worry the record store clerk who came by to check on me, and then I bought it and took it home. I didn't actually listen to the album for a few weeks, but every morning – and every time I felt off during the day or night – I would dig it out, stare at the cover, and feel a little bit better because I could see myself. It was strange to be able to

37

see myself – though obviously not exact, but the closest I've found – outside of my own head. It was strange, but also beautiful. Two weeks after I bought the album, I got a copy of the vinyl record – still without having listened to it – because it had bigger art.

I put the vinyl copy on the wall beside my bed. Since I often woke up in the middle of the night or in the morning feeling confused, I thought it would be helpful to have the photo right there as I woke up. This was especially important because I was living in an apartment where one wall of my bedroom was a mirror and waking up to the sight of how I looked to others instead of how I looked to myself was often difficult. I even slept holding the CD album cover some nights when I was feeling especially lost or nervous or depressed. I don't know how, but it was very comforting. This is how I became a big fan of Kacey Musgraves long before I ever bothered to listen to any of her music, and why there are so many fingerprints all over the album covers of hers that I possess. If I ever meet her, I plan to say thank you and freak out at seeing an image of myself that is not me walking and talking in front of me.

***

The second most important funeral in my life happened in 1998. It was also the most important funeral I attended because I did not go to the one that probably shaped my life the most. It was the twelfth funeral I was eligible to attend. It took place in my hometown. All my family, even members of Mitchell's side of the family from Texas, showed up for the occasion. I didn't talk to any of them. I didn't like any of them at all that day. I didn't even want to attend, and after the event, I wished I would not have attended.

My oldest sister was the most important influence or role model on my life when I was a child and a teenager. She introduced me to positive examples of what she called "male crossdressers" in the early 80's – what we thought I was as a kid, she didn't have much information on other options back then – in the form of Alice Cooper, Prince, David Bowie, and others in the music world. She introduced me to positive forms of bisexuality as well and shared (and maybe initiated) my deep, never-ending crush on Michael Stipe. She started and helped me build the music collection where I took vacations from the rest of the world. She would drive me around the city, blaring some hair metal or Hootie and the Blowfish, and tell me about all the wonderful things I could be no matter what anyone else said. She taught me how to "borrow" books from bookstores without their permission, and how to hide sensitive – read bi, trans, lesbian, gay, and liberal – things in a little cubby in my bedroom she helped me build. Most of all, she may have been the first person that actually saw me, not the versions of me I put on to live, but whatever real me might exist behind the masks.

She had been out having oysters with her husband on the night she left the planet for whatever happens after our lives end. He was drinking. She was the driver. There was a storm the media at the time called one of the worst in a long time. He was the first partner she had after getting out of an abusive marriage. She loved him. He actually treated her well and loved her too. They were happy. She was happier than she had been in at least a decade by my count at the time. They left the oyster bar in her car. He was too drunk to drive. She was probably sure the storm was no big deal since they often weren't a big deal no matter what the news said. There was water on the roads. It was at dangerous levels, the news said. The lights on the highway that ran along the river went out that night. Nobody knew why. My oldest sister's car left the road right after one of the few lights on that road. It hugged a tree moments later. There is still a cross on that tree even though she didn't believe in that stuff. I answered the phone that night. I was scared to answer the phone again for a couple years.

**

The last gift my first love gave me was a yellow hat. I went to some concert at the end of the 1990's, and the singer was wearing a yellow hat. I don't know why or remember who the singer was, but I fell in love with the hat even though I thought the band was terrible. After Gillingham died, I wore that hat a lot until I lost it in a fast food restaurant in 2003. I still have a picture of it.

I was meeting some friends for pizza and pasta, fast food style, on the day my hat disappeared. It felt like I lost more than a hat, but I guess the heart will do that. We were sitting around the table laughing and making fun of some television show that doesn't seem all that important right now. The friends aren't even all that important since I don't think I knew any of them for much longer after that, and I wasn't close to them for more than a few months before that day. I put the hat on the bench beside me while I ate. This was something I always did. I didn't like to eat with a hat on, and in fact, I didn't particularly like wearing hats in the first place. I liked wearing that hat. I felt like some part of my lover remained in the fabric of that hat. It was a symbol. Symbols were important, especially in that relationship. This was because only five other people ever knew about that relationship while it was happening, and two of them were already dead along with Gillingham by that day at the fast food place in 2003.

I almost caused a car wreck seven minutes after leaving the restaurant. I was riding with another friend who almost hit another car when I started screaming that we had to go back to the fast food place. I had forgotten my hat. I startled everyone. They were surprised I cared so much about a hat. I didn't tell them why I cared so much. We went back to the restaurant. We did this after five far-too-long minutes of discussion about the hat and why I cared so much where I did my best to come up with a cover story I can't recall now. We went back to the restaurant, but the hat was gone. I spent an hour asking questions about it. No one said they knew anything. Hats don't walk. It did not just leave. It wasn't in the trash. I checked. It wasn't on the floor somewhere under the booths. I checked. I spent the rest of the 2000's trying to find a yellow hat to replace it, but I never did. I still miss my hat.

CHAPTER 7

There was a scarecrow in the field behind the vacant lot near where I grew up. It was in the middle of some of the rows of planted vegetables and fruits. I would stare at it for hours thinking up stories about what it had been before it came to the field. I would make up fantasies about what our world looked like to whoever was inside those clothes.

***

Stirring her coffee, Susan says, "You may be the nicest, sweetest person I've ever met." Three days later, over another duo of coffees, Miranda says, "How can you be such an asshole, you don't seem to give a shit about anything or anyone." A week later, over cheap beers in another part of town, Ronald says, "Are you like the meanest motherfucker ever, or what." Two months later in a bedroom that smells like weed, Jamie asks, "Are you just broken, like too fucked up to ever be nice or sweet or kind?" I wonder if they're all right.

I don't know if it was intentional, but my entire life seems to have played out in isolated clusters where I – accidentally, purposefully, I don't know – gravitated toward interactions with people in different groups so I could be a different person in each group. This may have been due to necessity. I was bisexual. This meant I could be hated by gays and straights, or I could play gay at times and play straight at other times and save my own sexuality for times where I was with other bi people only. I was non-binary in terms of appearance while also always knowing I was a trans girl, once I learned the terminology that is, as well. This meant I could slide into men's, women's, non-binary, and other trans groups at will wearing different appearances. I was also an orphan that was adopted, which meant that, according to what little science concerns such folk, I didn't necessarily have the same familial anchor other people did and was thus always looking for who I was or might be. I was also agnostic, which meant I annoyed the hell out of the gnostic folk whether they were theist or atheist and confused the hell out of the religious folk whether they were spiritual or atheistic in their rituals. It seemed like I was always somewhere between what people expected, and for some reason, this led me to try on many different selves.

It was not, however, the whole line of scientific literature on dramaturgy that led me to these endeavors. I did learn about such things, and even became one of the people who study such things in my late twenties, but I think it was high school that first exposed me to the ways one can play with other people's assumptions and need for stability. It started with an accident that I didn't bother to correct. I was a sophomore in high school. We had to have identification cards at my high school. They made me one with my first name. They made me one with my middle name. They made me one with one of my nicknames. They made me one with another one of my nicknames. I was just going to the office where they made the cards to get out of class, and saying I lost my card and needed a new one seemed like an easy excuse. In the end, I had four cards with different names on them. I started wearing them at different times for fun.

This began as an internal joke, but by the end of the school year, I realized that people would come tell me things about the me that used a particular name without knowing I was the same person. This fascinated me. I was four different people. Some people knew one of me. Some people knew another me. I wondered how far I could take it. Trying to find out, I stopped using all but one of the identification cards, and started rumors about all three of the other versions of me that people had become aware of throughout the year. As I expected, people would come to me – the me identification card I was using – to try to ascertain the nature of the rumors. I could decide what was true, and what was false. I could share this information with whoever asked, and then enjoy when the rumor came back to me from someone else. This worked even though there were people in my grade who had known me throughout school because no matter how many times said people tried to convince others that I was one person, the others would not believe them. They knew the version of me – and the name attached to that version – that they had met in person and trusted that over any other information.

**

I love open houses. Let me be clear, I do not love them because I want to own a house. I honestly don't care about property, aside from my books and records. I could care less if I ever own a house or any other large piece of property. I can see the good. I can see the bad. I just don't care. I will likely only own a house if my life partner decides that is something they want to do at some point. I do not love open houses because people are selling houses. I like open houses because they are a perfect opportunity to try out different lives.

I figured out this hobby when I was 29 years old. Obama was in his second year as president, and many realtors in Florida were attempting to come back from the financial crisis. As a result, many of them started doing more open house events. I probably would not have known or cared about this normally, but I was in graduate school and a friend of mine invited me to one of these events where there would be free food. We went. We ate. We also had fun by pretending to be a married couple with a child – a four-year-old daughter named Madonna thank you very much – looking for a home for our soon to be growing family. I was John. My friend was Ginny. We were in the market and had questions about everything. We wanted to know about the safety of and schools in the neighborhood. We were curious about the events in the neighborhood, and the demographics of the community. We were concerned about long term costs related to maintenance and renovations we had already planned to make on our new home. We were at the place long enough to have two meals from the buffet.

After that day, I realized that I enjoyed playing the character at the open house more than most social activities. It reminded me of all the different versions of myself I played on dates, in friendship groups, and in many other contexts throughout my life. It was fun, and especially at a time where I had the security and opportunity to be more open and out about a lot of aspects of myself that had been more hidden in the past, it felt like a fun way to stay in touch with my past. As I did as recently as three weeks ago, I started going to open houses fairly regularly. I would be Diana in search of an infinity pool because my wife had back issues. I would be Gerald in need of a good neighborhood for my three children to play safely in the front yard. I would be Dakota who was worried about "those people" – never say which people, it's more fun this way – and seeking to be calmed by the owners, realtor, or both. I would be Trixie with the fresh new bachelor's degree that made me want to finally move out of the hotel where I turned tricks. It was a fun game, and though there usually wasn't a buffet, I still enjoyed the experiences.

***

"Oh my god, Patricia, you have to check this out," Lauren squealed as she approached me in the back room of a club in Atlanta in the fall of 1998. That year had been especially tough for me in many ways. My oldest sister died, but we'll get to that. Another friend died as well. Gillingham and I broke up again for what seemed like the last time at the time. I was enjoying being multiple people at school for the third year in a row, but I was also realizing I was close to basically no one at school. These were difficult things, but one thing positive came out of them. I found the courage to spend some time living and appearing as a woman on the occasional weekend trip to Atlanta. I had done this before in small doses and even met a nice woman who taught me a lot about dildos, but I felt somehow more free and fearless in the face of my oldest sister's death. The way I figured it at the time, my days were numbered anyhow, so what did I have to lose.

Lauren was my best friend in Atlanta, but she only knew me as Patricia or Patsy. She didn't know that I had another name on my legal records. She didn't know that my body might not look the same as other people named Patricia when I was naked. She didn't know where I lived exactly, but figured, because I hinted as much, that it was a suburb of Atlanta. It was not. It was almost three hours away by car, and it took me a little longer than that each weekend I made the trip because there was a rest stop about halfway between my home and her home where I stopped each time for about three hours. Those hours included the time it took to transform my appearance and become Patricia in the eyes of others. It was not easy, but Kimber and my oldest sister had taught me well. I don't know how many, if any, people ever suspected anything, but for whatever reason, I didn't really care at the time.

I would rent a room at a cheap hotel, not unlike the one I would work at in Augusta a few years later and stay there for the weekend. I would tell my family I was off with friends for the weekend, but they didn't ask a lot of questions, so I never had to come up with much by way of an excuse to disappear for a while. Cell phones were just starting to populate my social networks, but we were well before the things could be used to track where we were at every moment as far as I can remember. I would check in at the hotel on Friday night, and then go hang out with Lauren and her friends. I did this accidentally my first trip that year by going to a teen club I'd gone to on an earlier series of adventures in the city, and meeting Lauren at the refreshments table. We hit it off almost immediately, and for the next year, her and Patricia were best friends of a sort. It was the senior year of high school for both of us, but our time together was much more important for me.

***

I don't recall ever having only one name. I don't mean the way most people have a first, middle, and last name. I don't mean the way many people have childhood nicknames. I don't mean something deep or metaphysical either. I simply mean that I always felt like there were different names running through my head no matter what people called me. I wonder if it has to do with spending the first part of my life with a family who called me by one name, the rest of my childhood with another family who called me by another name, and the bulk of my early education having one name on the official roll and another in practice.

I don't know the source, but none of the names I was called as a child ever felt right. I always felt like something was missing or that the people were talking to someone else. When I met my birth father Mitchell in 2006 and my birth mother, we'll call her Carly though we might call her something else by the end of this conversation, in 2010, they each called me by different names, and both of these names were different from the two – one at school, one at home and church – I was most often called as a child. I don't exactly know or understand – and even neuroscientists are not yet sure of a good answer, though there are some interesting hypotheses and theories out there – how we consolidate memories as young children, but I often wonder if that was the problem the whole time. Maybe, on some level, I remembered my names in Texas when I was in Carolina, and maybe the fact that neither place could settle on one name above and beyond others created confusion or some kind of natural fluidity in my young brain. I don't really know, but I still wonder about it.

What I do know is that from as far back as I can remember, I never felt the need to be just one thing. Since I had multiple names, or at least felt like I did, it made perfect sense to me to see names, labels, categories, and other markers as purely symbolic and flexible. I developed similar understandings – not all that uncommon in much artistic and scientific theory I learned when I got to graduate school later – of things like race, class, gender, sexuality, religion, age, and other, what many theories call them, "socially constructed" beliefs and rituals. Even as a small child, however, I remember wondering if it was that I couldn't accept just one option that made me feel like I was always between the labels instead of part of one of them, or if it was the opposite. Maybe it was a natural development in between other people's labels and ideas that created the recognition of the multiple names and fluidity inside my brain. I have no clue, but maybe I'll figure it out or stop caring someday.

CHAPTER 8

You know you are a terrible writer when your best friend will not even read your work.

***

The first word I said to my current best friend was no. They were a student in one of my classes. It was eleven years go. I was a graduate student instructor. They wanted to learn how to study people the way I was starting to do for a living. I wanted to leave because class was over. They asked if I would teach them to study the world by observing and analyzing what people did and said. I said no.

You have to understand that I found them especially annoying. They kept asking questions that only sometimes applied to the course. They kept saying the word "like" fifteen million times in the middle of each of these questions. They were, just by looking at them, into the Greek life thing that seemed a whole lot like idiocy personified to me. I mean, other than some wonderful blowjobs from supposedly straight, likely closeted bi or gay, frat boys in college, and some awfully tasty baked goods made by sororities at my undergraduate institution, I never found anything interesting about institutions built on conformity, lack of originality, superficial notions of womanhood and manhood, and strict sex-gender segregation. The fact that these places could exist, much less thrive, on college campuses was my first indication that being smart, creative, original, or otherwise better than anyone else in terms of merit had nothing to do with who went to college in my country. I have yet to see anything, by the way and despite individual exceptions, to suggest otherwise about Greek life or colleges in general. Simply put, I was fairly certain my one day best friend was a daft kiss-up I would be best served by ignoring as well as I could. So, I said no, and then I said no again a couple more times.

After saying no enough times to where the question itself was beginning to annoy the crap out of me, I finally said what the hell. Instead of intending to actually teach this annoying student anything, however, I devised a practice exercise that – as others have agreed – would send anyone who wasn't incredibly serious about learning running for the hills. Since the student flinched every time any of the words bisexual, lesbian, gay, or transgender were used in class, I instructed them to attend an LGBT event in town. Since what they wanted to learn how to do takes incredible patience, observation skills, and willingness to write constantly, I had them attend the event without any way to take notes, without any instructions, and without any preparation. They were as overwhelmed as I expected. Then, they had to come back from the event, and write a detailed summary of the event – multiple pages mind you – from memory. It was an impossible assignment, but one that would give them a taste of my work. It was actually the same thing one of my own mentors who later became a friend did to me in undergrad.

At the time, this turned out to feel like a very unfortunate miscalculation on my part. Due to their flinching, I assumed that, like many people in the Greek system I've met before and since, they were at least somewhat – intentionally or otherwise – bi, trans, or homo phobic. The flinches, it turned out, were coming from the opposite direction. They were closeted without even yet having reached the point where they knew they were closeted. Due to the average writing ability and requirements in contemporary colleges, I also assumed they would balk at a multiple page assignment with no resources or instruction. I was incorrect again. They had been writing in journals, just like me, for their whole life, and enjoyed the experience. They did the assignment. The work was terrible, but it was terrible because the assignment was impossible not because of them. In fact, it seemed like the kid had potential. I remember trying to convince myself it would be okay to lie to them about that so I wouldn't have to teach them.

Nikki convinced me not to do that because she enjoyed having the little annoying kid around at the event. Nikki was my primary life partner at the time, but we'll talk about her more later because one time I told her the truth when I probably shouldn't have and that was why she was in Florida with me at the time. As I often did, I followed Nikki's advice, and started teaching the kid, we'll call them Gibbard from here on out. Almost two years later, they graduated and were no longer my student. I was happy about this, but I was also surprisingly feeling like I might miss working with them. I tried not to think much of it until they asked if we could stay in touch. I was angry with them at the time for lying to me about something – I know, talk about the irony – so I almost said no again. I said yes instead. Eleven years later, and I'm really not sure how, they have become my best friend, though they still annoy the shit out of me.

***

I had my head between Kimber's legs the first time I realized she was probably my best friend. I was fifteen. She was eighteen. She had probably been my best friend my whole life, and until we lost touch in the early 2000's, she held the title. She was also the only one of the four people I have ever considered my "best friend" that I was sexually active with at any time. I don't know why that is, but for some reason, I have generally developed my closest friendships without sexual components since the days Kimber and I spent together.

I don't know why I was thinking about this the first time I performed cunnilingus. It was the first time with Kimber, and the first in my life. I don't know why I was thinking about friendship at the time. It might have been because Kimber was a little jealous of the person who would become the one I considered my best friend after Kimber and I lost touch. It might have been because – other than Kimber's carefully worded instructions before, during, and after the fact – I had no clue what I was doing between her legs that morning. Since having no clue led me to start thinking about all the ways I could be doing it wrong, maybe I just wanted something else to think about so I could enjoy the experience. I don't know why or how I came to the conclusion at that time, but Kimber stopped moaning long enough to giggle when I surprised her by raising my head and saying so.

I remember being fascinated by the sound of moaning even the first few times I heard it. I didn't care about the vocal range or the gender identity of the person involved even back then, but something about a human moaning felt like music to me. It still does. I was also fascinated by the exploration – ongoing, with detailed notes and log files as of now – of the variety of human bodies. Thanks to Kimber and Gillingham, I had basically begun my own intro courses in map making and the like by the time I reached the middle of my teenage years. I remember the biggest surprise was just how nuanced, complex, and varied bodies and bodily reactions could be to different types of pressure, motion, and other variables. After putting my head back down and slowly shifting Kimber out of giggles, I shifted from consideration of what constituted a best friend to these other factors for the rest of my latest sexual educational session.

***

My first best friend, even before Kimber, mind you, was a painting of a child in a blue hat staring at the water. I don't know what the painting was called. I don't know who painted it. It was on my wall in my bedroom, I think, before I got there. It was captivating. I would sit and stare at it for hours and it would, with my help, tell me all about its day. I think I was four years old when I destroyed it, but time is hard to tell for me in the blurry years of my earliest youth.

I should note that I didn't know I destroyed it until about a year after I did so. I did it by accident. A childhood misunderstanding accomplished by a child who was misunderstood. I thought the child in the painting was me, or maybe some version of me. I don't know if my little mind was capable of that abstraction, but I thought it was a painting of me. It was not a painting of me. In hindsight, it did not even look to me much like I looked to others or I looked to myself. It was not me, but I thought it was me and thought can be a powerful thing. In this case, it was so powerful that I thought the painting was missing something. I don't remember thinking this, but it is the only explanation I can come up with after the fact. I added something. I added it in pink crayon. I like pink crayons. I added one of my names. I wrote it backwards because I did not yet know how to write. It wasn't my best work.

I found out this was a problem a year later when my mom noticed the crayon in the top-right corner of the painting. "What did you do," she asked. I said I signed it because I thought it was a good painting of me. I actually said picture, but I don't think I knew the difference yet. Anyhow, I said it felt lonely without a name, so I gave it one of mine. She was not pleased. Dad was not pleased either. My sister that was older than me, but younger than my other sister thought it was hilarious. I didn't understand what the problem was. The painting went away after that – maybe to some farm where it could play with other paintings. I never saw it again, but I still sometimes think about it because it was the companion I shared my first honest conversations with, and I wonder if the loneliness I thought it had was actually my own.

***

My third best friend, the one after Kimber who was after the painting, brought a gun to my first wedding. This was, you should know, not her fault. Nikki and I realized that we would save money and could try out our feelings for each other if we got married. We also figured out how to trick our families into paying for it, and for two honeymoons we enjoyed to varying degrees. The problem was that my best friend at the time did not realize we were joking when we worried how the families would respond to each other, to our Muslim and fellow Queer friends, and just to the day in general. She had a gun thanks to her job as a junior Jack Bauer type of government employee, and so when Nikki joked that she should bring it, she did.

The wedding was at a chapel in Aiken, South Carolina. It was a tiny affair that was followed by a more crowded reception at the home of one of Nikki's many family members. I ruined the wedding by wearing a black shirt. My dad was angry about the cake. Our friends were bored so they stayed outside on the porch of the house for most of the party. Neither of us enjoyed the party, but it was the price we paid for the cash and gift cards. I liked my black shirt and so did Nikki. Nikki was my first spouse. There is a joke one of my undergrad professors used to make about his first wife that I want to put here, but I promised Nikki I never would say that joke about her so you'll have to wonder about it or find me in a bar where Nikki can't hear us. This might be tricky since Nikki is the reason, along with my former student who we will talk about later, that I kind of almost have multiple best friends at once right now for the first time. She also has a long memory and a fireball temper so maybe I won't even tell you the joke in a bar where I am sure she can't hear me just in case.

We returned the favor – doing something important at my then-best-friend's wedding that did not involve a gun – a few years later. My best friend of the time was getting married in one of the cathedrals in Washington D.C., and she thought it would be hilarious to have, as she put it at the time, "my non-believing ass" read the Biblical scripture during the wedding ceremony so we, as she and Nikki agreed, "could finally find out for sure if sinners ever did get struck by lightning." I stood there in a place where a president's funeral took place long ago. I read the words from the epistle. I watched for the lightning, and I could tell by the looks on their faces that Nikki and my best friend were too. I was actually a little disappointed when no lightning arrived in the end, but I guess I'm used to being disappointed by fictional characters.

CHAPTER 9

"You know what the problem is," ze says laughing and tossing a finished cigarette on the ground outside the Marta station in College Park, "There are two kinds of people in the world, and we're neither of them."

***

Trudy was the best friend I never met. I saw her speaking at an event in Columbia, South Carolina in 1998. She was beautiful, intelligent, funny, and smart as hell. She was also the first trans woman I ever saw share her story of life in the south, transition, and sexual fluidity. I didn't have the courage to talk to her, but sometimes, I wish I would have.

At the time, I was fairly certain that transition was the only way I would ever feel whole. I never had the certainty that many other people I have met over the years have, but I was as close as I've ever gotten at that time. Thanks to the use of a rest stop on Interstate 20 between Atlanta and Augusta, I had found a way to occasionally spend some time living as a woman, and I was more and more certain that I wanted to do it full time. Gillingham and Kimber were both supportive, but I had no clue how to go about such things. I went with Gillingham to an event for bisexual and transgender people, two words I was only vaguely aware of at the time and could not yet define well, where we saw Trudy and others bravely speak about their experiences in front of a crowd of other scared kids and adults trying to survive. It was the first time I ever called myself bi and trans, and the first time I realized there really were other people out there like me – it wasn't just something Gillingham, Kimber, my oldest sister, and a couple zines and books I found said to make me feel better. It was amazing how important that piece of information was to me.

I had a similar experience in graduate school when I fell in what I would call friendship love, or maybe incredibly powerful crushing on a stranger you have never seen much less met, with three scholars. One of them had written a nuanced book on religion and sexualities – areas I wanted to study even though I still thought, despite Nikki's disagreement, that people like me did not fit or belong in the academy – that I ended up carrying around with me everywhere I went for more than a year. Something about the realization that someone had done that kind of work made me believe that I could. The second one I found when I opened an academic journal and read an article that actually took the violence myself and many other trans people face in our lives seriously. I ripped out the article, folded it up, and took it with me everywhere so I could read it anytime I felt afraid of the cis majority that was other graduate students and professors that I interacted with on a daily basis. The third one wrote another academic article that was the first of these where I saw the word bisexual used in a non-evil manner, and I began to follow everything she did. I'm pretty sure I understood the importance of representation before these experiences, but I know these experiences drove home the message more than I could have put into words at the time.

***

All I can see is a shaved arm pit and an immaculate piece of art decorating a shoulder. I am terribly frightened. There is no immediate reason to be frightened. She is washing my hair. That is her job. I am enjoying the feeling of the hands in my hair. I am still afraid.

I am afraid because in a few moments she will be using scissors in close proximity to my body. This may sound like an odd thing to terrify a grown human, but bear with me. When I was a child, my mom was a hairdresser. Not surprisingly, this also meant that she did my hair and my dad's hair. She was our barber. She was paid to do this so paying someone else to do this for us seemed crazy to her. She said that, more than once. The problem was that my mom had no concept, that I could ever ascertain, of diversity. She imagined that whatever worked on my dad – or other people – would work on me. The problem here arose because I have a very sensitive body for some damn reason. This comes in handy at times, but it means some things that should not be all that painful – like having hair pulled by a certain type of scissors or razor – can be incredibly painful and, I would guess due to the fact that I'm in my late thirties and still scared of getting my hair cut, potentially traumatic.

I remember, though I'm sure this is not an empirical reading of the situation, sitting in the chair in my childhood kitchen as if it was a prison cell designed to torture me every time I got my hair cut. The stylist puts a towel around my neck and leads me back to her chair where the scissors live. I want to run. I want to hide. I want to scream. I look at my spouse. They seem calm so I try to relax. I start humming songs I like in my head, and imagining the stylist is a friendly elephant telling me a story. It works, well, it works well enough to get the job done. The only difficulty, once my stylist is an elephant holding a storybook instead of a human holding scissors, is that there is a mirror in front of me. I don't like mirrors. I hate them. I don't look like me in the mirror. I look like what other people see when they look at me, and this makes me feel like I don't exist. I avoid the mirror. I fixate on the products on the shelves nearby. I keep humming and imagining the elephant. It will be over soon. I will be back later. The elephant has lovely tattoos.

***

The first time I realized how upset I was about life was when I almost killed someone. It was 1995. I was fourteen years old. I was not a violent person then and am not now. I was angry. I was too angry. He was a kid from my school. I don't remember his name. He said something I don't remember that pissed me off for a moment. I hit him. He hit me back. It should have just been the classic schoolyard fight between too overly excitable kids.

Somehow, sometime after those first couple punches, I lost control of myself. I don't know how it happened. I don't remember how it felt. I knew almost immediately after the fact that it was a problem. I scared myself. I scared the other nine kids around us. I don't know what I did exactly. All I remember is that by the time two of my friends pulled me hard enough that I started to lose my grip on the boy who said something that angered me, his face and head were bleeding and I was within inches of smashing his head into the concrete sidewalk. That would not have been good. I remember they pulled me even harder, and I fell back onto them. I remember looking down and seeing blood on my hands. I remember feeling especially scared that the sight somehow excited me. I wanted more of it. This was not good.

***

I'm fairly certain I had my first real crush that wasn't Gillingham or Kimber when I was nine years old. It did not go well. This guy in my class was nice to me. He was rich. I was not. He invited me over to his house to watch a new show called *Beverly Hills, 90210*. We watched the show. It was nice. I thought he loved me. I don't think he did. Even if he did, I'm pretty sure I made it impossible for anything to ever happen when he caught me breaking into his house.

I did not know how to handle someone liking me. I spent most of my time alone. The only people I really talked to – Kimber, Gillingham, people from baseball, people from basketball games – were not in the same classes I was most of the time. I was generally alone and quiet. I was okay with this until a boy invited me over to watch a television show. I did not know how to be friends. I did not know how to have a crush out in the open. I didn't know anything. Well, I knew one thing. I wanted him to invite me over again. I wanted to spend more time with him. I wanted to be his friend so I could have a friend. He liked the television show and baseball cards. I knew nothing about the former, but I had some of the latter. I didn't really care for them. They were just a way my dad and I could have something to talk about. It was the same reason I played sports in the first place. A few days later, after waiting to see if the new boy would call and noticing he did not, I mentioned baseball cards to him at school.

He invited me over again to look at baseball cards. I don't remember exactly what happened next, but by the end of the visit, we were in an argument over some stupid baseball related thing. I think the real source of the argument was when he told me he liked some girl in our class. I wanted to be the girl he liked. I did not know how to handle the sadness I felt. I thought I could show him I was special. This was not a well thought out plan. I snuck back to his house in the late-night hours, and found my way into the first floor, where his playroom and the garage were, through this grate I saw earlier in the day. It was loose. I opened it and slid into the home. This part went well. I stole one of his baseball cards thinking he would think he lost it, ask me about it, and then I could find it on my next visit. I would be his hero. He would forget the other girl. It was simple. Somehow this made sense to me. Somehow, I did not see the many gaping holes in this plan.

The plan did not work. Instead, he showed up at my house in the much less nice neighborhood a few days later. He accused me of stealing his baseball card. I remember, in a moment of utter hypocrisy, I admit, feeling offended by the accusation even though it was correct. Naturally, I denied the accusation. Naturally, he made it again. We argued. We argued some more. In the end, he left angry and told me he never wanted to play with me again. You would think that at this point I would figure out that I had made a mistake and try to do better, but that is not at all what I decided to do. Instead, I came up with another plan. It was another stupid plan, of course. I figured that I could sneak back in the house, replace the card, and then when he found it, he would like me again. He would come back to my house to apologize. I would pretend to be so upset but accept his apology after careful thought. I would be the bigger person, and all it took was one more attempt at breaking and entering. What could go wrong?

Everything could go wrong. That was the answer that eluded me at the time. That was the answer waiting for me when I slid back into the grate that night to replace his baseball card. It never crossed my mind that he might have figured out how I got in and stole the card in the first place. It never crossed my mind that he would be up late at night like I often was because for some reason I assumed other kids followed their parents' rules. It never crossed my mind that I would be on my stomach with my feet having just made it through the grate and find myself looking up to see him standing over me. "I found your card," was all I could say.

CHAPTER 10

My therapist says I talk too much, but she only says this when we're in bed together. This leaves me uncertain as to whether or not to consider it a medical opinion. Maybe I'll ask her next time.

***

I probably should not feel proud of myself for giggling at the sound of the Mormon missionary I just slept with crying in the bathroom as he cleans himself up. He is fearing eternal damnation. I'm planning to steal his magic underwear. He was decent in bed. I didn't care. I only slept with him for the underwear. He is not my first missionary. He won't be my last. He is not my first Mormon either, but that is beside the point, I think. I giggle some more as his sobbing grows louder. I'm not sure what this says about me. I put my clothes on, put his underwear in my purse that some say I should call a bag when I look like a man, and leave.

I went through a phase in my early twenties. This phase involved collecting religious artifacts from religious people I slept with in dirty motel rooms. I don't know why I did this. Maybe it was my own way of speaking back to the church I was raised in. Maybe it was some anti-religious anger I needed to let out in a productive – though not reproductive, mind you – fashion. Maybe I just have a sick sense of humor, and I should be ashamed of myself. Maybe I would be ashamed of myself if I was capable of such nonsense. Maybe I would be religious, come to think of it, if I was capable of that particular brand of nonsense. I don't know, okay, I just enjoyed it. It was a fun hobby. It was a way to pass the time.

Whatever the cause, I spent a few years doing this. I would keep an eye out for missionaries, preachers, imams, rabbis, nuns, priests, and any other "obviously religious" people that might be fun for a roll in the hay. I kept my own scorecard. It was like that Pokémon thing, I wanted to catch them all. I especially enjoyed collecting souvenirs when possible. By the end of the phase, I had a nun's habit, three different priest collars, two pairs of Mormon underwear – one for males and one for females, I was disappointed there was no set for intersex folk – and a Book of Mormon autographed by a famous elder, and far too many crosses and sets of prayer beads. I used to keep these items, except for the collars and one pair of the Mormon underwear that I wore occasionally, in a box. I would look through them some nights reliving the attempts to convert me, the tears the religious men often shed after sex with me, and the handful of fun times when I saw one of them out in public after our activities.

**

When I was in high school, there was a Baptist Church just outside of town. Gillingham and I would drive out there because there was nothing around for miles. It was in the middle of the woods between our little town and the next little town forty-minutes further down the road. The church was especially nice because the parking lot was set in the back of it. This meant that the church was on the deserted road, and the parking lot was even more anonymous. Gillingham and I spent many nights in my truck bed touching each other under the combination of the stars and the large cross on top of that church.

When I look back on it, I'm somewhat amazed by how many times I had sex in and around churches in the 1990's. I'm even more surprised by how many different churches I at least made out in during the same decade. I thought this was odd until I learned similar stories from a wide variety of other people after I started studying religion and sexuality for a living. I think the only way I've been able to make sense of it is by remembering that churches were often the only places where we were left completely alone as kids. Alongside that pattern, there is the fact that churches are often deserted at times when no event is scheduled. The two of these things together basically turned churches into the closest thing to hotels and apartments a bunch of teenagers of various sexualities and genders could get a hold of at the time. I don't know how we all figured this out at exactly the same time, but it seems like it was common knowledge. If you wanted to be alone without your clothes with more space to move around than the average car could offer, you just went to church. It was simple.

I remember so many times doing things that would make baby Jesus cry in churches. Each time, without fail even when I tried not to, I found myself imagining Jesus watching on some satellite television style hook up. In my mind, he was going blind rather than crying, and we were basically his own personal porn stars. There was the pornographic film where the kids get to giggling over alcohol in the library and accidentally start a threesome. There was the one where the kids, because of *Melrose Place*, skip volleyball to play with other types of balls. There was the one where the kids use the back pages of a Bible to roll joints, and then snuggle under the cartoon depictions of Biblical stories on the wall while craving a big bag of Doritos. The genres and subplots were endless, and I always wondered who might win if Jesus ever did some pornography awards based on all the sex we had at his house.

***

I always get turned on when I hear "When the saints go marching in." This may seem odd, but you have to understand that there is a perfectly logical reason for this correlation.

I was in ninth grade at the time. I was attending a football game at the high school because that was all there was to do on a Friday night. I was hanging out with a girl from my church that was rumored to be sexually active and interested in me. I don't remember her name, but I do remember she was fun. We were laughing with some other friends, and I asked her what she thought of intercourse. I had done all kinds of sexual things by this point, but I had not had intercourse with a female. I thought it would be much more fun than the game. I was right about that, and lucky that she agreed. Together, we snuck out of the stadium, and made our way up to the classroom buildings behind the stadium. We were hoping to use a classroom, but the doors to the buildings were locked. We tried three of them. We had no luck. I remember saying maybe we would have better luck another time. She didn't like this response. Instead, she suggested the breezeway just outside one of the doors. It didn't look comfortable, but we were young and bored so that didn't matter all that much. I said sure.

We got into the most comfortable positions we could on the concrete breezeway. We used our jackets for a makeshift bed of sorts, and she had protection so when I realized I did not it was not the end of the road. She said she had been planning to catch my attention if there was a party after the game. We actually both caught other people's attention at the party after the game that night. In fact, we never caught each other's attention in quite the same way again. I don't think either of us were all that impressed by the other in the breezeway. In any case, we made the best setup we could, and began to have some fun. We were really getting into the heat of the moment, for lack of a better phrase, when the band on the field started playing "When the saints go marching in." We both started giggling, and then we kept going. I think of that moment every time I hear that song.

***

The first time I met my life partner's neighbor was the last time I ever saw her. I am happy about that fact. I'm sure she is happy about that fact. I know my life partner is happy about that fact, though I don't know if they ever saw her again. If they did, I don't think they were naked when they saw her again.

I always enjoy it, to varying degrees, when an inside joke becomes a reality. Okay, I might not enjoy it in the moment, but over time, it is kind of fun to think about. My life partner and I had a running joke when we were first getting to know each other in my early thirties. Since we both enjoyed having the blinds open at their house, we kept joking that it would be funny if someone randomly stopped by one night and got a kick out of us making fun of each other, dancing to 80's music, or doing whatever else we were doing in the living room. This was funny because it was seemingly impossible, or at least, very unlikely. This was because there were these massive bushes outside the house that almost completely blocked the windows. For someone to see inside, even if we drew the blinds completely, though we never did that, they would have to stand in the middle of the bushes, lean into the window, and look inside. We laughed at the thought that anyone would do such a thing until one fateful night.

We were, well, how do I put it, mid-coitus on an armchair we both enjoyed. It was just another night. We were not doing anything unusual for us. We were having fun. Then, without any warning, there was a loud knock on the window. We looked up and saw a woman who lived in the complex staring at us through the window. For some reason, she started pounding on the window again. Then, as if that wasn't enough, we heard her make her way to our front door and begin pounding on it – I would guess – as hard as she could. She did this for three minutes while yelling that we should be ashamed of ourselves for doing what we were doing. Never people to be ashamed of sexual activity consented to by the parties involved, we found this part of her tirade hilarious even in the moment. We also wondered why she wasn't ashamed of herself for going into a random set of bushes to spy on her neighbors. We didn't ask.

CHAPTER 11

I was raped when I was 16. I didn't tell anyone other than Gillingham until I was 30. I'm not over it yet, and I don't know if I ever will be.

***

I only tried to be a race car driver a couple times. It did not go well. It was fun. It was scary. It was probably stupid to race on an abandoned dirt track in McCormick, South Carolina with a bunch of drunken friends in the middle of the night. The track didn't have lights. We didn't have any safety equipment. I'm surprised none of us got hurt.

We would ride out of town to the woods beyond our town. We would go as far as we could on gas that, back then, was only about a dollar per gallon. We would roam around the varied contours of the Strom Thurmond Lake. We would dig through the abandoned churches and dirt roads on the sides of Sweetwater Road. And sometimes, just to be a little bit more idiotic than usual, we would go out to the abandoned dirt track where races took place at some point. The first few times we went out there in the middle of high school, we simply got drunk on the hood of one friend's Mustang or in the bed of my truck. We smoked some joints, drank cheap beer, and when we needed something even cheaper, Thunderbird wine. We laughed at the sky and at each other. We didn't have anything else to do with our time.

The next few times, we held our own races. The track was in terrible shape – there were ruts everywhere that were not exactly easy to spot in the dark. There were patches of grass growing in at various places, and the occasional – almost as wild as us – animal roaming through the area on the way back to whatever it called home. The lack of visibility combined with the suspension issues that arise when you pass 70 miles an hour in beat-up, old cars and trucks, alongside generous portions of cigarettes, cheap wines, and weed, made driving around in circles yelling at each other much more fun than I think it would have been otherwise. Although it may sound like it from the outside, I don't think any of us were suicidal at the time, but rather,

I think, in fact, for myself, I know, we just never thought about how dangerous it was. Maybe it was our youth. Maybe it was the substances in our blood. Maybe it was something about having little by way of future plans or cash. I don't know, but sometimes what is dangerous only appears dangerous long after the fact. The midnight drunken races fit into that category.

***

My father taught me my first lesson in social science. He didn't mean to do this. I doubt he knew he was doing it. At the same time, it was one of the primary survival strategies I used throughout my young life. He taught it to me in the woods in the 1980's. It is one of the things I'm most grateful for, but I've never thought of a way to tell him that.

My father – the one who adopted and raised me, not the one I met in New York who donated the sperm for my conception – was not what anyone would call an easy person. He was generally angry. He was often sad. He was able to anger and annoy damn near anyone without much effort. I don't think he ever had any friends for very long that I ever saw. He was quick to offer opinions without any information, and even quicker to tell anyone what was wrong with what they were doing, how they were doing it, and what he somehow knew was the right way. This did not endear him to many people. I'm not sure if he cared. I do know he loved my mom, my sisters, and me, but in his own way. I'm not sure if that way was ever enough for me, but it mattered just the same. I've never been able to nail down if I think he was a good father because I think the answer is more complicated. In any case, he was my father, and somewhere between all the good and the bad he taught me something important.

We were in the woods because he liked to be in the woods when he was younger. I liked being in the woods as well, but for different reasons. We were in the woods because he wanted to show me a man's sport. I didn't want to be a man, and I didn't see the sport in killing animals, but I went along as young people do. We were in the woods because even as early as the age of five or six, it was obvious we had very little in common, and the woods could be a chance to bond. I didn't really care if we bonded, but I think he did and I still feel like he does. We were in the woods, and I was bored out of my mind waiting on an animal to arrive. He was having fun, somehow, and much more calm and friendly than usual. I remember thinking it was kind of a wasted day and wishing I had thought to bring a book or a comic when he said, "Now, I think I need to explain something to you, you got to understand camouflage if you're going to hunt." I nodded my head, not all that interested, and not yet aware this was, in fact, a very important lesson for me even though it had nothing to do with becoming a hunter someday.

"You know that scarecrow in the field with them vegetables, son," he said, and I nodded, "Well, that's a decoy meant to scare the animals so you gotta have it visible and out there in front of them, but camo is different." I can still hear the drawl in his voice when he spoke, though it has gone away some with age. "With camo, you kind of want to blend into your surroundings, but you don't want to over-do it because that could draw attention. You want to seem like you just belong there, even though course ya don't," he said laughing and smacking me on the back the way he often did then and does now on the rare occasion when I visit. "You just kind of set these here clothes," he pointed at what we were wearing, "And these screens right here," he pointed at the screens, "So it seems like you was always here, and none of them animals ever know anything different or scary is anywhere near them." He chuckles, "That way, they don't react, they just act normal and never notice you until you're ready to jump out and do what you gotta do."

While we were sitting in the damp leaves the next few hours and while we drove out of the woods without any new dead animals that day, I kept thinking about this lesson. I had no intention of giving a damn about hunting, but I was trying to figure out how to handle people at school, church, hell, everywhere, who seemed so different than me and often upset by how different from them I was. I asked my dad to stop at the bait and tackle shop in the woods about halfway back to our town. He did. I picked up a notebook for sale there. He said I could have it and asked the fella behind the counter for a price. It was a dollar. It was a cheap spiral notebook with an orange cover. He bought it and gave me a pen out of his glovebox. I started my first journal as we drove to town. I was crafting notes about how people acted. I was figuring out how I could camouflage myself as one of them. He was talking about Kenny Rogers. I was figuring out how to live as me without scaring others too much until I was ready for them to notice I was there. He never asked what I was doing with the notebook.

**

When I was 34 years old, I successfully freaked myself out in one of the more fun ways I have come up with to date. I had written some stories about fictional characters that were based on the combination of my own life and hundreds of interviews I did in the southeast in the 90's, 00's, and early 2010's. When I created these stories, I often pulled pieces of the world I grew up in, like other writers do, and moved them into other places and settings that were useful for the story. I was standing in one of these places, a park in Statesboro, Georgia of all places, texting my best friend thinking about the fact that I wrote a scene in this place where a main character meets up with their best friend for a chat (a scene that didn't make it through the editing process of the book). It was a surreal moment. I wondered for a moment if they would show up, the characters, or if maybe I was only a character in a story.

I used to think about myself as a character in a story quite often. There was a magnolia tree in the front yard of my childhood home. It was massive. It was pretty. My mom was allergic to it. It was a pain in the ass to rake for extra cash. I would sometimes sit underneath the branches for hours imagining adventures taking place in the tree that I could watch in real time if I could just find the way that the author hid them from me. I would also think about what kind of sadistic author might have created my life. This may have been an early aspect of my inability to develop faith or spirituality of any kind, now that I think of it. I would play out similar adventures and imagine other unseen narrations taking place where I went as a kid. There was something comforting about these things long before I started publishing fictional works of my own. What I did not ever think about, until that day standing in a place I used in a story, was what it would feel like to be in a place that was both real to my senses and a place I created in a fictional realm at the same time. It was, well, odd.

***

The first time I heard a gunshot that did not take place in the woods I was looking through a stack of compact discs to see which ten I would give a friend five bucks for that day. He was in need of cash. I was in love with music. We were at his grandma's house. It was in south Augusta. It was a Saturday afternoon. We were newly met through a mutual friend I met the first week of high school. He was nervous about something. I never caught his name. Our mutual friend was eating some pork that he said was pretty good.

I don't think I knew what the sound was at first. It rang out loud in the quiet of the afternoon. The mutual friend hit the floor. The guy selling me the albums said, "Get down," and I did what he said as I watched him do the same. The grandma was at bingo. The sound came seven more times before the mutual friend and the guy selling the albums got off the floor. I didn't get up at first. I didn't know what was happening. I think I should have been scared, but I don't remember feeling afraid. More so, I was just curious. It was about an hour later when the sirens started going off in the neighborhood. The mutual friend and the guy selling the albums were explaining to me that what we heard was a shooting. I didn't know those happened in the city across the river from where I lived. Well, I didn't know until that day. They watched the street. They watched the police. They wanted to see what would happen. That day, nothing else happened. Well, I got some CDs, but otherwise nothing happened.

CHAPTER 12

I know you don't give a damn about this crap, but I'm showing you anyhow.

***

Some of my favorite childhood memories involved short trips over to Clearwater, South Carolina. My grandmother lived there, and my mom was raised there. It was a town that was somehow even smaller than the one I lived in back then. It was just a couple neighborhoods, a grocery store, and a McDonald's. Later, there was celebration when they got a Waffle House. It was the south so, of course, there were also fourteen churches. I would accompany my mom on days where she went over to Clearwater to get groceries for and hang out with my grandmother. We would leave our house, drive to Clearwater, walk through the grocery store, pick up McDonald's food, and go to my grandmother's house.

My grandmother had a roommate or two, other relatives, when I was very small, but I don't remember these people. She lived alone the whole time I remember knowing her. She was from the town. She worked in the clothing mill that shut down before I was born. She raised my mom, my biological grandfather who was my mom's brother and Mitchell's father, and one other child who was a woman to the best of my knowledge. Although they had a father, she raised them alone for the most part because their dad killed himself when they were young. I heard rumors, sometimes from my grandmother herself, that she killed him because he was an abusive prick, but I have no clue if this was true or just a story. Her oldest daughter, my mom's sister, also spent some time in an abusive marriage, but by the time I knew her, she was a different person with a handful of children whose names I still often forget. My mom's brother, my biological grandfather, left the town for the military, and later to move out west. He was the only one that left the area, but he was also the first one to die. He loved a fast food restaurant that was popular in the area where I grew up. It was called Krystal's. I don't know a lot about him. Well, I know that I, apparently, looked a lot like him when I was a child.

My mom stayed in the area but left the town after her junior year of high school. She married my dad that year, and moved to Augusta, Georgia. That was where he lived his entire life before they moved to a small town in South Carolina at the end of the 1960's. His own father that I barely remember meeting once or twice as a small child lived in downtown Augusta, but that house no longer exists. It was torn down and turned into a garden when I was in my teens or maybe my early twenties. Dad cut meat for a living. Mom cut hair for a living. Like most of the people I knew growing up, life was about cutting a lot of things – costs, time, needs, and wants especially – to get by and take care of the children. Mom and I would go out to my grandmother's house, and my grandmother would eat Little Debbie cakes, dip her tobacco, and tell me all kinds of stories about her life in the mills and in the south as young girl.

***

The last time I saw my birth mother, she was hooked up to machines in a hospital and very rarely knew who I was. She was just past 50. I was 33. I came in to visit, and as I suspected, to say goodbye. She was sick the whole time in my early thirties that we knew each other. She had cancer. I found this out when she showed up in Tallahassee to meet me and Nikki after finding me on social media. It was a cancer that was tied to vegetables and stomach lining. I can't eat most vegetables so that's a break in my favor, I guess. We were friends, close ones, for almost four years.

My birth mother was someone I kind of gave up on meeting before she found me. I spent years, as I did with my birth father, seeking to locate her. I looked for both of them when I drove out to Houston and the surrounding areas with no real plan in the 1990's and early 2000's. I looked for both of them when I had regular access to the internet during college. I looked for both of them in dreams and fantasies I had about other possible lives I could have lived. After a roller coaster of three years, for lack of a better term, knowing Mitchell, however, I wasn't as invested in finding her as I had been before. I also had almost no information on her before meeting Mitchell, and it turned out that Mitchell had very little himself. I was almost 30 when she reached out to me in 2010 – apparently, Mitchell helped by telling her I would like to meet her when she reached out to him first – and to my surprise, once given the green light, she drove out to Tallahassee to meet me. Mitchell never bothered to visit any of the places I lived, or at least, not yet.

I thought about this first visit, and how much fun it was to hear her version – at times different, at times similar to Mitchell's and to my parents' – of what happened back then. I got the impression that, at least in the narrative she constructed while I aged, she never wanted to give me up, but had few other choices since Mitchell's immediate family – other than a sister who was told no – did not want me, and her family was half disaster stories and half a younger sibling that could not have handled me. I remembered thinking about the various versions of me in people's histories of their lives repeatedly as I compared her version of events to Mitchell's version, to my parents' version, and to the versions I collected from various sources over the years. I'll never know what actually happened, but I enjoy the stories. We spent time together laughing, telling stories, and having dinner. I think I loved her.

I watched her body respond to this or that drug and wondered what would happen if we got or had more time. We got along much better than I do with most people, and by then, I was beginning to build a more stable life with my current life partner who would become my second spouse two years after my birth mother, who I even started calling mom alongside my other mom, passed away. I was there for just over a week. She was in the hospital about the same amount of time. She didn't die that week. I went home pretty sure she would die soon. She didn't think so. Her sister didn't think so. My life partner hoped they were right, but thought I was right. I was right. I would be back in Texas not much later for her funeral. I would be driving across the southeast to say a final goodbye on that trip, but we'll get to that.

CHAPTER 12

***

The least important, but most interesting, funeral I ever attended was my own. I don't mean that I died, and this is one of those things where a character writes to the audience from beyond the grave. I do not have the skills of Alice Sebold so I will not likely write that novel myself. I'm a fan of Alice Sebold, but that is beside the point. I mean that I learned that other people thought I died. I learned this fact at a funeral that was otherwise uneventful.

It was one of the funerals in the mid-twenties on my list if you're keeping score, but a few of these blend together in my mind so it's hard to say which one was which numerically. I think this was 34, but I'm not sure. It could have been 33 or 35 – those three are hard to separate. It was for a friend who got too close to a windshield in the middle of our twenties. She and I dated for a little while in high school and did more than just date a few drunken times in my early twenties, but mostly I remember her as a friend without the benefits because that was her primary role in my life. I don't know if her death affected me at all, to be honest, but finding out I was dead was a bit of a surprise. I thought I would have been the first to know.

I was standing in the back of the assembled masses surprised that so many people cared this much for someone I never saw talking to many people at all. I was standing there by myself as I often did at formal events. I was hoping to not be noticed all that much. I was wearing a comfy pink skirt, and t-shirt the deceased gave me. It was an outfit she liked on me. I thought that was appropriate, given the circumstances. I was never sure what to wear to these events. The service was ending, and people were starting to move around. I was going to leave right away, but then someone called out one of my names. I turned and waved to the person I do not think I knew. She came up to me, and said, "I thought you died." I shook my head as if to say, "not that I know of" because it was about the only thought that came to mind. She said, "I heard you were killed in a car accident in Atlanta." I shook my head again. It seemed to be working well enough in the conversation so far.

I was honestly thinking she was just crazy. It was the best explanation I could come up with until she waved over three other people who thought I was dead. Apparently, there was a car crash in Atlanta a few years prior that took the life of someone from our hometown. Somehow, and no one seemed to know how, people became convinced that the "someone from our hometown" was me. This rumor spread like ones I spread about myself in high school. There were people that were really happy that I was alive even though I did not get the impression that we were going to suddenly start noticing each other in our daily lives. I mean, I didn't want to know any of them any more after my resurrection. I figured they felt the same. Still, for some reason, finding out I was not, in fact, dead long before that day was comforting to some of them.

***

The most interesting breakup of my life happened in 1994. I was dating, or whatever people do at the end of middle school that may involve making out and occasionally being driven somewhere by someone's parents, a friend of Yvette's that was by any measure one of the nicest, most interesting, and fun people I knew in my youth. This is not me being nice. I genuinely liked this girl, and I have enjoyed seeing her as an adult at times for a few minutes. I began dating or whatever her in hopes of avoiding Yvette for reasons I'll explain here at some point, but over time, I really enjoyed my time with her. She didn't ask a lot of questions. She was a lot of fun. She didn't know about my boyfriend and wasn't likely to find out. It was a good deal. Well, it was a good deal until two things happened in eighth grade. First, Gillingham got jealous of her – so did Kimber – and wanted me to end it if I didn't mind. Second, with the increase in genuine affection for her, I was feeling conflicted about the rest of the things I was doing without her knowledge.

Gillingham and I could not date openly. He made this clear. I agreed for the most part, but mainly because I was worried about getting hassled even more for being strange. I was still somewhat naïve about violence, though that would change in time. Kimber and I couldn't date openly because she was dating the boy her parents adored to keep them out of her way, and because my parents would not have accepted that relationship for many reasons having to do with age, reputation, and her lack of church ties. My official girlfriend, as the three of us called her, was perfect because she provided cover for the three of us to just be the way we were without hassles. This, of course, needed to be sorted out if I was going to break up with her. Kimber came up with a great plan.

First, since the girl I was dating was one of the good girls from my church, we set it up to where I could be alone with her one night. There was a big event that is not all that important to this story, and we had a chance to hang out alone after it. Like many "normal," as Kimber called them, good pre-teens, my official girlfriend had hinted about sex type stuff, but that was about it and there was no indication she was interested in or ready for such things. As such, Kimber suggested I talk about sex that night in graphic ways, and at some point, do something utterly stupid – flashing my genitals and asking how they looked was what Gillingham came up with – that would almost guarantee a conversation – and potential rumors – on the subject later. I did both of these things, and to my surprise, the girlfriend was cool and there were only minor rumors within her friend group. It was disappointing because we figured the rumors would get me hated by her parents and end the relationship while also providing my parents with a reason why maybe they shouldn't want me dating in the first place. I would be free.

It didn't work, but then Kimber came up with another idea. We were talking on the phone one night, and I mentioned that I hated that damn clicking sound the phone made when someone else picked up the line. She asked if that ever happened on the phone with my official girlfriend. I said yeah, all the time. Her parents, I'm guessing, and our next plan confirmed, wanted to know what she was talking about with the potentially bad kid in the other neighborhood who was over at the house sometimes. Anyhow, noticing this, Kimber told me to talk about sex – graphically again, of course, but also in ways I would never actually consider doing things as if I was on a porn set or something

– next time I heard the pickup. I was nervous. I said she had a little sister who was nice, and I didn't want to upset her. Kimber convinced me to do it anyway because if it was the little sister, she wouldn't understand anything anyway. I didn't think this would work. Kimber did. Gillingham thought it was hilarious.

I didn't know if I would do it until I did. It was more fun than I expected. The girlfriend again handled it better than I expected. She was pretty damn open minded. Her father, however, was on the other end of the line. He was not pleased. He didn't even wait a single day. He showed up at my house explaining – in what I could call a yelling-based rhetorical style – that I was a scary, dirty pervert – maybe, but not for the reasons he thought – that should stay away from his daughter. My parents acted deeply offended. They promised to punish me. The father of my now ex-girlfriend, or so I thought, left. My parents suggested I be careful about hanging out with that girl now. They also stopped asking why Gillingham and Kimber were around so much after that day – mission accomplished. Well, not entirely because the official girlfriend now wanted to date me in secret. I told Kimber and Gillingham, and to my surprise, they had a newfound respect for her. They agreed it was cool, and so I started seeing her again while still feeling conflicted about all she didn't know. We lasted a few more months.

CHAPTER 13

There were many times I went to the field beyond the vacant lot near my home when I was a child. Most of these times I went to talk to the scarecrow. It wasn't because I found its outfits all that interesting. It wasn't because I enjoyed the Wizard of Oz all that much. It wasn't because the corn stalks were comforting. It was because I could tell it my secrets without fear. I told it so many secrets over the years that it may have been the best source of knowledge about me. Of course, that didn't do anyone other than me any good.

***

The worst thing Kiley ever did was wait until after I sold most of my record collection to destroy the records I loved the most. This was also probably the best thing she ever did. I sold over 92% of my collection – I did the math – because that, alongside living with my parents again for a few months and taking a crappy job at a coffee shop for those months, allowed me to afford moving to Florida for graduate school. I kept 8% of the collection because those records mattered to me the most. Kiley made sure I would not have those records either. I was not happy.

I don't even know if I can fairly blame Kiley for what she did. I still do so, but I wonder if it is fair. The whole thing happened because Kiley and I had a little disagreement that I never let her know about in the two years I enjoyed her body and the body of a nice guy during college. She thought of herself as my college girlfriend. I did too. The disagreement came next. She thought being my girlfriend meant that I was not sleeping with someone else, and that we had something serious that would build into a long-term relationship. I did not think it meant either of these things. I thought it meant I didn't have to bother getting laid in college because she took care of those needs for me as part of me smiling when she said we were a couple. I didn't tell her I also had a college boyfriend because, well, I never could see how that was her business. I mean, it's not like I thought of our time together as anything serious.

Because she did think of our time together as something serious, she did not react well when I told her I was moving to Florida for graduate school. She finished college long before I did, but she had no interest in moving. She was also unhappy because she was hearing rumors – that I did not confirm or deny – that I was dating some guy. I was dating some guy, but I didn't want to know what she thought about that. She told me anyway just in case the rumors were true. I didn't care. What I did care about was my record collection. I was, in some ways, losing my mind over having to sell most of it off to raise money for first month's rent, last month's rent, security deposit, and food money until the first paycheck in Florida. I was also unhappy about having to move back in with my parents for a couple months, but I was very happy they suggested it and appreciative for the help. Without it, I would have had to sell the whole collection. In hindsight, this might have been less painful.

Instead, I came home to the small cottage I rented in the backyard of another house. I came home to find every compact disc and vinyl album I did not sell broken into thousands – I didn't count, but it had to be thousands – of pieces. There were also notes, and some other broken things, but none of that seemed important. I stared at what was left of what had been my most prized possession, and quickly did some real-world math. If this was her reaction to me moving away, I didn't want to know how she would react to a full break up. As such, I decided to wait until Thanksgiving – when I would be visiting from Florida, and more importantly, when none of my stuff would be in Georgia or South Carolina or simply within her reach – to end the relationship. I cleaned up the fragments of my record collection, continued packing for my move back to Carolina across the river, and planned exactly how the breakup – with minimal collateral damage – would transpire months later.

***

I distinctly remember the day I learned to miss people who were not yet dead. It was a random September evening in 2012, and I could not get my life partner out of my head. This was especially bad because

I had recently learned that I broke up with them – I still don't recall doing it, but the information has been confirmed multiple times from varied sources – at the end of the summer. This was probably a PTSD style reaction where I blacked out and ran away from caring about something too much. At the same time, I learned what it felt like to miss someone that I could theoretically talk to again. I have felt the same a lot since. I'm not sure I like it.

What nobody ever tells you is that missing people is fucking terrible. It hurts. It aches. It will not go away even if you know you are going to see them again soon. It feels a lot like grief but is not quite the same. It doesn't give you any warning, either, no, it just sneaks up and smacks the shit out of you. I am still getting used to it, which I guess makes sense considering that I didn't get to feel this way until I was 31. At the same time, I sometimes wonder if I want to get used to it. I sometimes think it would be much better to forget how to do it. The problem is that this is not possible because it is, in my case, triggered by my life partner, and there is no way I would give them up unless I was forced to by death or them choosing to want something else in life that doesn't involve me or some other force beyond my control. Put simply, I don't know if I can like missing people, but I also have no way to avoid it anymore.

That, I think, is the interesting part of this new lesson. Throughout most of my life, I was able to avoid missing anyone because no one ever really knew all of me. I lived so many lives, wore so many faces, moved in and out of so many different circles, and kept so much to myself that no one ever knew more than a pizza slice's worth of this pie that is me. This was incredibly effective for me, but it also meant I was always a little bit lonely – not great – and also always a little bit down the path where I would leave whoever cared for me – great if you're terrified of intimacy and feelings. It was an intricate dance that I think might have to do with all the deaths I experienced, something inside me that remembered being abandoned as a small child, or some other source that I had no conscious knowledge of at all. Whatever the case, I lived a life where no one knew me, and I missed no one – not even Gillingham or Kimber – unless or until they were gone for good and out of reach. Now, however, there are people who are starting to know me, only a few, but still, and that apparently means I get to know what missing someone – and even more than just one person – feels like.

***

One of the best things my oldest sister ever did for me involved theft. I read a lot even as a kid. I did not come from a rich family. I did not live near the library. I did, however, live near a bookstore that I could walk to many times per week without trouble. This, my friends, was where my oldest sister came in – she taught me how to steal books from the shop, read them without messing them up, and return them to the shop without getting caught. Thanks to her lessons, I had a limitless library at my fingertips from the day I turned eight.

The shop was in a string of stores that included a pharmacy – that also had books – and a grocery store – that also had books. I would go up to the shops fairly regularly throughout my I-cannot-drive-yet-so-my-ability-to-go-anywhere-is-limited life. I would study the magazines, especially the ones about makeup, dresses, and music, and I would often buy a cassette tape – usually a single – from the book, magazine and record shop. I would also move through the books while grabbing two of them – one the owner could see, the other I was hiding with my body – until I made my way to the back of the shop. At the back of the shop, I would place myself directly between the mirrors in the corners of the ceiling. I would then look at my fashion and makeup magazines while sliding a paperback book under my shirt and between the waist of my too-big shorts or pants and my body. I would then spend at least fifteen more minutes looking through the magazines and stop by the cassette rack – after putting the book the owner saw me grab back on the shelf – on the way out of the shop. As my sister instructed, I made sure to get a cassette at least once out of every three visits so it would appear that I was simply a kid checking out magazines and buying music.

As I got older and made some cash from yard work and later jobs, I bought more than my fair share of books from that shop and the bigger bookstores across the river. At the same time, I continued working the system my oldest sister taught me when I was a kid in the 80's. I would steal one and buy one. Then, I would return the stolen one, and stay to read a third one. I would then repeat this cycle every time I visited a bookstore until, for some reason, I finally stopped doing this and started only borrowing or buying books when I was seventeen. Maybe it was because I associated the technique – and the luck that led me to never get caught – with my oldest sister. She passed away when I was seventeen, as I'll talk about later, so maybe, somehow, her absence made the system no longer feasible in my mind. I don't know. I don't remember stopping, but I do remember realizing I had stopped at some point later.

***

The worst thing Roman ever did was remember my name. He was 20. I was 15. We were intimate a few times before he left for college. He went to college in Upstate, South Carolina. I didn't bother to listen when he said where. That was my mistake. I was in Greenville, South Carolina when I saw him again. I could have ignored him, but he remembered my name.

I was walking with a woman named Gia who was showing me around her body and her hometown that summer. We were at this coffee house that was kind of underground, but not all that special otherwise. I would return to that same coffee house in my thirties under very different circumstances. That is not part of this story. Roman was going to school and living in Greenville. I didn't know this. I probably would not have cared. I did care when he passed Gia and I on the street, stopped, and said my name. This was not necessarily a problem because Gia knew I dated boys, girls, and people who were both of these things. She found out by accident when she caught Gillingham and I kissing in the woods. We thought we were going to die, as if she had a whole crew ready to jump us right there in her pocket. She did not. She didn't care. She was bi too, but no one knew about her like no one knew about me – read a choice friend or two only. The same type of no one knew about Gillingham as well, but he was gay not bi, so it wasn't exactly the same experience.

No, Gia didn't care that this random guy with the 1950's Elvis kind of hair knew me in an intimate manner, but Roman's friends cared a lot. He was going to a school I had never heard of at the time. It would become famous in the years to come for training anti-LGBT zealots and funding George W. Bush. His friends knew his past, but he was saved now. This made me a problem – a demon if you will – that he had to face. He chose to face this demon by slamming me into a wall, and I felt about three punches from him and his friends before the fact that Gia was especially talented in martial arts made the whole ordeal end much better than I'm sure you can guess it could have. All I remember was Gia's body becoming an impossibly fast blur of moving limbs, and the next thing I knew, there were Bibles and Bible-thumpers spread all over the sidewalk. I stepped on the middle of Roman's back as I took Gia's hand, and we continued our stroll through the city. I would be back the following year without her, but that's another story for another time.

CHAPTER 14

Chinese Democracy *is the best Guns N Roses album. There, I said it.*

***

The first time I heard the word terrorist the older white guy who said it was talking about me. He didn't know that. I didn't tell him. In truth, I didn't know his name then any more than I do now. He was sitting at the bar of the local diner near our neighborhood. He was angry. I was having a milkshake. It was sometime in 1988, but I only remember that because he mentioned the year while ranting about the terrorist kids that forced him to go to the hardware store.

When I was a child, I lived in a home on a corner lot in a mostly white working-class neighborhood. I was very small when a high school boy with cute calves who lived on the next road over started talking to some of us younger kids. His name was Malcom and he reminded me of Butch from the *Karate Kid*. He was friends with a high school boy that lived in the house at the end of my road – the other corner lot. I hung out at that house sometimes because that high school kid had a brother closer to my age and a sister about my age. In the middle of our block, there was an old guy who always yelled at all the kids whenever any of us ventured into his yard for this ball, that Frisbee, or some other thing. We thought he was an ass long before I heard him call us terrorists that day.

One day, Malcom came up with a great way to get the old fella who always yelled at us back. His mother had given him a bag of fireworks, and we were in the middle of the road setting them off as darkness came for the night. As the sister of the high school boy on my block set off the latest bottle rockets in the group, Malcom suggested we set some off at the old guy's house. Well, he said, "Not at his house, but in his mailbox." Being young white people of a certain age with little to no parental supervision in the eighties, we thought this sounded like a wonderful idea. Malcom and the other high school kid bundled up a large stack of the fireworks and tied the fuses together so they could all be lit at once. I was drafted as the "smaller kid who can run away faster without being seen" that would put the fireworks in the mailbox. I did this. I lit them. We watched from a little ways away, maybe two houses. The sound was loud. The mailbox was gone. We didn't plan that, but it was hilarious. The old man came out in his robe screaming and cursing. We hid. We did it three more times.

***

"Hypothetically," I say walking into Donny's room, "What would you do if you had the chance to sleep with an ex that was fun in bed." Donny is my roommate. Donny is from Waycross, Georgia, and thinks Augusta is way too big of a city after three months here. Donny is a good Christian boy who I met when we were matched up as roommates in college. Donny will only stay a year before going back home. I like asking Donny moral questions because I will leave out important details, take his answer, and then do what I want. Later, I will tell him about it, and with the added details, he will agonize over the advice he gave. I don't know why this is fun for me, but it is. I like to tease the nuances of stated morality.

"Hypothetically," I say to Martini sitting in a coffee shop in downtown Augusta, "What would you do if you had the chance to sleep with an ex that was fun in bed, but the ex is in a relationship and still cares about you so doing so might lead to some not so good things for them since you are definitely not getting back with them." This is the same question I asked Donny, but this time I added more detail. I asked Martini because he is also a good Christian boy. He will talk about such things with Donny. Donny said go ahead. Martini said no because it could hurt the other person. I went ahead, but I would have done that anyway. The point here was to set up a conversation between the three of us on the porch the next night after I had already gone ahead with what I was going to do anyway.

On the porch the next night, Donny, Martini and I are having drinks when I tell Martini that I went for it because Donny said it was fine. Martini then turns to Donny, and in asking why Donny thought it was okay, he mentions the details I didn't tell Donny. Donny then backtracks and agonizes over what he now feels was bad advice. I know he will pray about this later. Martini is laughing. Donny is repeating, "Shit man, I didn't know." I'm enjoying this. When the humor dies down, I ask, "Hypothetically," but before I can say anything else Donny says, "Oh no, not again," and leaves the porch. Martini almost falls down laughing.

***

I was sixteen years old when I learned what the Confederate Flag actually meant. It was 1997. I was dating a guy named Jamal. We were dating in secret. This was because we were both supposed to be boys, at the time. This was because I was white, and he was black. This was because we lived in South Carolina. This was not uncommon for either of us at the time. The first time Jamal came to my house, he taught me what the flag was.

I don't mean that I had never before been told about the flag. I lived in South Carolina, remember, so the flag was everywhere. I was visiting recently and noticed that it still is. You will see it on highways, in cemeteries, on front porches, hanging from the backs of trucks, and even on many businesses where I grew up. It was out more when I was kid – it was even sold at side the road stands – and it remains a common sight now. It was also part of the curriculum in school. In eighth grade, for example, we had a course on South Carolina History where they taught us the flag was "a symbol of state pride and a reminder of the importance of the War of Northern Aggression." The War of Northern Aggression is what many of my books in school called the Civil War when I was a young lass in the 80's and 90's. Even if you could ignore these things, you would still see the flags on the publicity materials for bands like Lynard Skynard, Alabama, Hank Williams Jr., and the like. You would also see it on t-shirts, bumper stickers, belt buckles, and all kinds of other accessories. The flag was everywhere, but its actual meaning was much less likely to come up in conversation or classrooms.

Though it is embarrassing to say so now, I thought it was a symbol for Hank Williams Jr. when I was a kid because that was the main place I saw it. There was a popular version of the flag – that I had, that many white kids I knew had, that a few black kids I knew had, and that was hanging on my wall without me realizing how offensive (read racist as hell) that could be until Jamal told me so the first time he came to my house – that had Hank Williams Jr. in the center of the flag and advertised his name and a lyric from one of his songs on the top and bottom. The flag itself was the background for this Hank Jr. poster, I guess, in much the same way it was the background for where I grew up. Ironically, Jamal knew this version of the flag because his dad had the same one on their wall at home when Jamal was younger until one of his dad's siblings made him take it down. Jamal explained that the flag was a symbol of segregation, racism, and even the KKK. I didn't know any of this despite how much I read and my experiences with the N word earlier in life. I didn't even remember when or how the thing ended up on my wall. I took it down right away. I also tried to talk about it with my family and other people. No one wanted to hear it. They got pissed off at me for telling them what I learned. Jamal told me this was normal. He expected me to break up with him when he told me. I did not. Instead, we burned the flag in the field near my house later that day, and then went out for milkshakes.

**

In the years since leaving Georgia-Carolina to attend graduate school in Florida, I haven't spent much time where I grew up. I go for occasional visits. They generally last less than a week. I did this more while Nikki and I were together because she wanted to see her family. I still enjoy seeing the place, but I have little desire to do so more than, say, a few times a year or for more than a few days. I don't know what this means.

There are things I notice about the place now that were hard to see when I was living there – whether full or part time – at other points in my life. These may be observations due to age, education, or something like that, but they may also just represent the usefulness of distance and the experience of seeing many other places. Nikki agrees with me on such things after living away from where we grew up and then moving back to live there as an adult. She lives there now. In any case, there are things that seem so obvious now that were hard to notice back then. There is, for example, the terrible air quality in the area. As a kid, the air just seemed like air, but now that I have lived in other places where it is easier to breathe and there are not the same smells everywhere, I wonder what they put in the air in that area.

There are also the customs in the area that seem odd now. By customs, I don't mean the rituals around holidays or that kind of thing, I just mean the normal everyday things people do. One of the big ones is the way people talk, but we'll get to that. The biggest one is that everyone seems angry or sad most of the time. They smile. They shake hands. They ask about the weather and your mama, but they seem sad in their eyes. The body language sags for some reason. It is almost like the heavy air weighs down things in the area beyond the natural environment. Some of the bars are as full on a weekday afternoon as they are on weekend nights full of partying. Most of the people in the weekday crowd are folks who don't have jobs or barely survive on the wages of bartending and fast food. There is a silence that encapsulates everything, and it feels darker than it did as a kid. When I say darker, I don't mean the thing where a city person has trouble seeing in a rural neighborhood due to the lack of streetlights, though that is true here too, but rather, something feels darker. It feels like a sadness embedded in the place, maybe passed down for generations, that speaks in every silence as people move this way and that from this country road to that watering hole.

CHAPTER 15

There is a deer with a limp that runs through the neighborhood at night. It has been a part of the neighborhood since I was a small child, and I wonder what it would say about us.

***

In the middle of my third decade of life, I think every white person should spend time living in a predominantly black neighborhood. I don't mean passing by these neighborhoods on the way to the airport and stopping for a soda. I don't mean a couple nights in the middle of a vacation. I don't mean a random weekend when there is a farmer's mart that just happens to occur in such a neighborhood. No, I mean move there for an extended period of time – at least six months or a year would do it, I think – and live there. I say this because – without realizing it at the time – doing so in an attempt to find affordable housing earlier in my life was one of the most educational things I ever did, and it's an education most people I have met who are white need if they are ever going to see and work against white privilege.

You must keep in mind that Black people already know what it is like to live in predominantly white areas. Black people know what it is like – I've yet to meet or date or know one that didn't know this – to be the only dark-skinned face in a sea of white faces. People who even appear maybe Black spend much of their lives forced to go into such places for survival whether they want to or not. They already know what it is like to be on a train platform, in a store, on the side of a road in front of a house, or anywhere else with an endless see of white faces staring at them, and sadly, in many cases, wondering what they are doing there. They already know what those eyes feel like, and they have – even if a white person has been privileged enough to avoid seeing it for any of a million reasons – seen people pull their bags closer, their children closer, and otherwise suggest they are worried for no reason. Hell, we even have to have an entire movement simply to point out that Black Lives Matter because, for the most part, the vast majority of white folk in the country do not seem to already know this.

This is why I propose a program where any white person that was not born into a predominantly black neighborhood should be required to live in one for a while. I want them to know what it feels like to be the only face that looks like yours on the train platform, in front of the pharmacy, on the side of the road in front of a house, at the coffee shop, or anywhere else. At first, as people who appear Black have said for years, this is a jarring experience, and can often be rather stressful. This is something white people need to feel. Then, as many other Black people have noted throughout the years, you get used to it, learn to navigate the stares and confusion of others, and go on about your life the best you can. This is also something white people need to feel. These are things that every person who appears Black that I have met – whether or not they identify as such – has experienced and felt in white spaces at some point in their lives. Like any other privilege, however, this is something that most white people I have met – whether or not they identify as such – have not experienced. This imbalance is one of the many ones that should be changed if we seek to understand each other better.

This may also have more broad benefits. It is hard to ignore that Black Lives Matter – much less have to be told this by (mostly Black) people risking their lives for basic human rights and simple fair treatment – when those lives are Tommy, you know, the kid who taught you how to set off fireworks at that picnic two years ago. It is hard to ignore the importance of a life when that life is Natalie or Natasha, remember, those girls who showed you the way to the coffee house the first time you got lost in your new neighborhood. What about Brian, remember him, the guy who slung drinks at the coffee house while working a second job and trying to go to school, or maybe Jarard who sells you the cigarettes at the convenience store in your neighborhood so he can put food on the table. What about Bay, you remember him, the one who got into school because his single mother worked two jobs to make sure he could go to all those after school prep programs so many white kids go to before college. When the people who appear Black are people in your life, in your neighborhood, in your home, it is – from what I have seen so far – much easier to remember just how much they matter.

* * *

Shonna taught me about dildos in a dirty apartment in the Little Five neighborhood of Atlanta three months after the first time we kissed and danced together during one of the scariest nights of my life. She was a lesbian. I didn't know what the hell I was at that point. She was kind. I was scared again, but much less so than the other time. She was knowledgeable on the subject. I was mostly ignorant. She was gentle. I was shaking at times. She was talented. I would become so after some practice according to progress reports from others since. She was still interested in me after being the first person in Atlanta to realize I had a penis under my skirt. I didn't plan for anyone in those bars I was visiting illegally to know that.

It happened in the most innocent of ways. We were dancing. Other people were too. We started kissing. Not the first or last time that happened when I was Erin instead of Edwin for the night, week, or however long. We were dancing close and kissing. This was dangerous territory I was generally more careful about long before I was ever taught by a redneck het dude that I needed to be so careful. I wasn't as careful as usual. There was something about her auburn hair and strong forearms that captivated me the same way Gillingham and Kimber did. It was not a safe situation, but I got lucky. We were dancing close and kissing, as I said. She pushed me against the wall. It was wonderful to feel her power. It was terrifying in the next moment. She put her hand between my legs in the middle of a deep kiss. She was surprised. I was worried about dying. She tried to speak. I tried to run. It was too loud. It was too crowded. I learned an interesting physics lesson – five seconds can feel like 27 million eternities in the right context.

I separated from her as she tried to ask me something. She moved too slow. I got away and made my way outside. It was dark. I was scared. For a second, I couldn't remember where I was. This was the terrifying, lucky accident that led to my dildo education. In other circumstances, I would have turned right out of the door, and been blocks away before she made it outside – 22 seconds or too many eternities to count after I got outside if you're keeping score at home. I was not that fast. I couldn't remember which way to go. I may have had a panic attack. I say this because I was on the ground trying to breathe when she found me. I don't remember sitting down. It was not the smart thing to do. It was not what I had planned to do if I was ever in this situation. It was also a dirty-ass city sidewalk. I don't know why I thought her hands had transformed into swords, knives, guns, baseball bats, or something else equally dangerous to my continued existence, but I thought so as she reached out her hand and I flinched and curled in on myself. I remember wondering if anyone in my family or in my hometown would miss me. I remember feeling more sadness than I expected at the realization that I really didn't know the answer. I remember the dirty-ass sidewalk ruined my skirt.

If you recall, I was curled in on myself. The next thing I recall, she asked if I was okay, and miracle upon miracles, she didn't sound angry, murderous, or whatever people were supposed to sound like right before they killed me. It is funny the impact tone of voice can have on a person. I felt stupid as I did it, but I did it. I looked up at her like she just asked me to figure out quantum mechanics in the next five minutes. She somehow read the look perfectly. She said, "Of course you're not, I'm sorry, come on," and then, surprising myself again, I let her help me up and lead me toward an apartment building nearby. I honestly thought she just didn't want to commit murder right there in front of other people on the sidewalk. I thought that, but I walked into the dark alley with her anyway. I really do think I had a panic attack. It was like I had no control over my body. She sat me down on a bench in the alley – one many people used for a smoking space before, during, and after their adventures at the bar. She ran her hands through my hair – maybe sizing up where to make the cut in my throat, I remember wondering – and said, "I know I can't help you feel less afraid, and I'm sorry you have to feel that way, but I won't hurt you, you didn't do anything wrong Erin and there is nothing wrong with you."

If this were a movie, I feel like I would have something smart to say here. Instead, I blurted out, "What," without even realizing I was doing it until the words left my mouth. She kissed me on the forehead, and said, "You're not my first woman with secrets, sweetie." I remember clearly that I just stared at her. "Does anybody know," she asked softly rubbing my cheek the way Kimber did when I was upset. Her eyes reminded me of Gillingham's the first night we slept together. I shook my head no. She said, "And no one needs to," kissed me softly on the forehead again, and then after hesitating for the first time I was aware of, again softly on the lips. The next thing I knew we were kissing again like we had been before she grabbed me in between segments of a conversation where I talked about being afraid and she talked about her previous experiences with people like me. Over the next year, she would teach me all about dildos, but that night she taught me how to feel okay as a woman with another woman even in cases where our clothes might disappear.

***

Though I spent much time in the field near my house talking to the scarecrow, the most important thing the field ever taught me was the resiliency of corn. I was in my early 20's. I was driving a golf cart my adoptive father got for some reason. I was not supposed to be using the golf cart. I didn't care about that until later when I had to clean the thing to remove the evidence that I had used it. There was corn everywhere.

I may have mentioned that people grew vegetables in the field near my childhood home. One of the main vegetables was corn. I don't know why people wanted so much corn, but it was often the most common vegetable in the field. I enjoyed walking between the stalks when I was out thinking about this, that, or the other thing. Well, one day I decided – because, I don't know why, maybe there was no reason – that the fact that I was not supposed to use my dad's golf cart was the perfect reason to use it. I was always doing that. I would be told not to do something, and almost automatically, I wanted to try it out. This was no different. I did not care about golf carts. I did not even notice there was one on my latest trip to the childhood home until I was told not to use it. My dad was using it to pick up my niece and nephew from the elementary school – the same one I went to – in the neighborhood. Otherwise, I had no clue why the hell we had the damn thing in the first place.

In any case, I decided I must play with this golf cart. I took the thing over to the field because I thought it would be fun to drive it way too fast down the dirt horseshoe-shaped-track that went around the vegetables. I don't know why I thought this would be fun, but I did. It was fun, well, it was fun until I lost control of the damn thing and flew into a row of corn at full speed. This, sadly, was not the bad part of the story. Nope, the bad part came next. Corn, apparently, can be split into a billion pieces on impact. It can also go flying in a wide variety of directions. It can also land damn near everywhere no matter how small the space. These lessons were my reward for driving into a row of the stuff. It was everywhere. It was all over – and in – me. It was all over – and again, somehow in – the damn golf cart. It was everywhere. A thirty-minute joy ride in a golf cart led to almost four hours spent cleaning corn out of every nook, cranny, and yes, orifice of both me and the damn cart. I hate corn.

***

The most interesting thing my birth mother ever told me may be the reason for my first memory. I have had the same first memory for as long as I can remember. I blame this memory for my difficulty navigating small spaces and spending much of my life outdoors. I also blame this memory for my difficulty connecting with other people, though I don't know if that is all that realistic. The memory, in my conscious mind, began as a dream that kept happening when I was a kid. It was a nightmare. I would wake up crying or screaming or both. It felt more real than other dreams, well, except for the snake dream, but we'll get to that. I was much older when I realized that it was likely a memory rather than a dream. I still don't know about the snake dream, but maybe someday I will figure that one out too.

I'm going to start with the dream so that way you can try to figure it out for yourself if you want. That way, you can also decide if – like me – you think the memory I have and the story my mom told me is the same event. Ready? Okay, so the dream starts with me pounding on something above my head. I don't know what it is. I feel very small. I can't see anything, but I feel like I'm in a box. This terrifies me. I test it out the only way I can. I try to touch open space to the right. There is a wall there. I try to touch open space to the left. There is a wall there as well. I already know I'm flat on my back on something very hard, and for some reason, very itchy. When I realize I am in a box, in the dream that is, I begin to scream with all my might until I cannot make sounds anymore. I think I keep screaming without sound, but I'm not sure because by this point in the dream I'm shaking and cold. I feel more and more cold. I think maybe I pass out, but I'm not sure because I always wake up at this point.

Okay, there is the dream. What do you think? I think it is my first memory because of what my mom told me when I told her about the dream. She thought it was a memory. She thought I was remembering a specific night when I was less than a year old. On that night, my birth father, remember Mitchell, we'll call my birth mom Carly from here on out even though I might have called her something else earlier in this conversation, I don't remember, do you? Anyway, we'll call her Carly, I like that, it should work, okay, got it? Anyway, Mitchell was taking these energy pills that made him a bit paranoid, and on that night, I was crying a lot because I had this inner-ear thing as a kid that made me sick a lot. I was crying, and it was freaking him out. Carly was at work. Mitchell, as the story goes, locked me in the trunk of his car to get some peace and quiet. Carly didn't know how long I was in the trunk, but that was where she found me when she came home that night. I was in the trunk of a car, and by the time she found me, I was asleep – or maybe passed out – and shivering. That's it. That's the story. What do you think?

CHAPTER 16

Turtles…coffee…stuff…taco…booty…I not bad…I repeat these words multiple times every day in my head and often, when I feel close to someone, out loud. I generally just say or think one of them – without any other words for context or meaning. I don't know why I do this.

***

The best day Boston and I ever spent together was the one we spent stranded on an island. It wasn't a deserted island. It wasn't something like you see in the movies where we just missed the boat or fell off another boat. It was Hilton Head Island off the coast of South Carolina, and we were stranded because I didn't think not to take my truck keys with me when I went swimming in the ocean about an hour after we got there.

The day began like so many others. Boston was working in a diner just outside of my hometown, and I was at the diner having some coffee and grits. Boston and I were friends for years who occasionally slept with each other. We might have officially dated for a while, but I don't remember. She had a lovely son, and I helped out with him sometimes. She was coming off the third shift after working all night. The son was with his father. She had the day to herself to do whatever she wanted. I was bored. We decided to ride down to the coast for the day. It was only about four hours, at most, and we could come back that night. We didn't plan to get stranded with our combined $33 dollars. We didn't plan to meet a lovely locksmith named Al who drove us all over the island so her family and mine could wire us money after he learned that my truck had the type of ignition key that could only be replaced at the dealership. Did I mention it was a Sunday? Did I mention it was Father's Day? We had to wait until the next day to go onto the mainland, and get a key made at the dealership.

We also didn't plan for our families – it was toss up, we agreed on the way to use the payphones to call them – to come through with enough cash for a hotel. We also didn't plan for them to send us enough to have the nicest dinner out either of us had in years. We also didn't plan to have sex in the hotel pool that night. We also did not plan for this sexual swimming session to be caught on camera because we didn't notice the pool was under surveillance until after we had already finished having our fun. We also did not plan to find a pile of free CD's on the beach when we took a random walk later in the evening. We also didn't plan to giggle when we heard someone wonder aloud where their CD's went while they were at the restroom at a bar near the beach about two hours later. We didn't tell them, if you're curious. We also did not plan to sleep on the most comfortable bed either of us had ever known that night, but it was a definite bonus. We also did not plan to get back to our own lives, and long for the time we were stranded on an island.

***

The last time I went to college turned out much better than the first two times. I don't mean that I went to college three separate days, but rather, I went to college three separate times in my life and in three different ways. The first one didn't work out so well, and neither did the second. The third one, however, was the start of a journey to a Bachelor's, a Master's, and a PhD. I'm still surprised I even have one of these things.

The first time I went to college was almost automatically after high school. I disappeared out west with some friends who were silly enough to believe we could be a band first, but that didn't last very long. I did enjoy the ride, but I don't know what happened to the rest of the crew from that short-lived adventure. My parents, despite suggesting they thought I was not college material and investing much more money to make my older-but-not-oldest sister the first college graduate in their family, gave me $500 bucks for school. I accepted it. I told them I would use it to go to a nearby tech school. I went to the school, but not to more than one class. I visited a class where some guy in a tie was attempting to explain the common myth that there were only two sexes and decided to use the money some other way. That other way involved moving to a trailer in the middle of the woods with two friends, but we'll get to that.

The second time I went to college was, I have since learned, potentially illegal. I was in my twenties, and often bored with whatever job I was working. I was taking these trips with a trucker named Marty. I'll tell you about that later, but the important part is that one day when I was wandering around New York City while Marty did whatever he did between the rides south and north I met a cute guy named Gary who lived near the Columbia University campus. Gary was adorable, and there was something about the pigeon-toed way he walked that excited me in many ways. I started "dating" him without telling him that I actually lived in South Carolina, and only came north on trips with a trucker. I would stay at his apartment while I was in town. He would think I was too busy with work during other times. He thought I lived in Jersey because I told him that, and he was afraid of New Jersey, which was why I told him that. While he was at work one day, I rambled over to Columbia and sat in on a class.

I kept doing this, pretending to be a student like I saw some character do in a television show at the end of the 90's, for a long while on each trip. I would answer questions, and even do the readings for some of the classes. I was amazed by how easy it was, and until someone became suspicious about never seeing me outside of class, I kept doing it. To my knowledge, Gary had no clue. To my knowledge, no one at Columbia had any clue except for the annoying white boy from every Abercrombie advertisement who got suspicious. Going to college was more fun than I expected so when I stopped going to Columbia, I started going to NYU instead and I started going to the tech schools and the university back where I lived. I kept this up for much longer than I initially planned simply because I occasionally learned a thing or two. It was amazing to me just how easy it was to put on an "insert name of college here" shirt, carry a purse that others would call a messenger bag, and have people assume I was a student too.

***

The eighties were almost over when I first met someone who looked like me. I don't mean there weren't other people who had similar skin tone, hair color, or that kind of thing. I mean that every other kid I met seemed to have some adults that had, for example, similar body language, similar facial features, or similar voices. I didn't have that. The closest I had was a picture, that I later learned was of my biological grandfather, of a guy with similar facial features to my own. I would stare at the picture for hours. I was nine when I got a real-life example. She was some cousin from Texas, and she showed up at my grandmother's house.

Her mother was in the kitchen talking to my mom and grandmother when I found her in the backyard. She was playing with a ball, I don't remember what kind, and looked very sad. She was sad, I learned years later, because her parents were talking about breaking up. They would do this at some point without me hearing about it. They were visiting because her mother wanted advice. I didn't know this at the time. I didn't know that her mother was the sister of my birth father either. I didn't know I had a different birth father than my everyday father yet. I just knew she looked like me. This might be why it bothered me that she was so sad. I spent the afternoon talking with her about Texas, but I don't recall what was said. All I remember was staring at her and hoping to do so as long as possible. It was strange to realize, at least consciously for the first time, just how lonely I felt before that day. I was out of place. I didn't know how. I didn't know why. But on some level, even as a small child, I knew.

***

There was a road in between the town where I grew up and the even deeper woods and smaller towns near where I grew up. It was called Sweetwater, but I never bothered to learn why. It wound in the shape of, well, a snake is the best description I can offer. It went from an area called Trenton to a small town called Edgefield. It was very narrow at many places, and likely a terrible place to try to see how fast a Porsche could go. We did this anyway.

We didn't actually have a Porsche, per se. One of the guys in our casual friend group had a step-father, current mother's boyfriend, I'm not really sure, who had one. He would leave it parked in the front yard of the friend's mother's house every night. He kept a tarp over it because there was no garage. He would spend weekend mornings cleaning the thing, and he would drive it around the neighborhood near my high school – the neighborhood this particular friend lived in at the time – for an hour or so on Sundays. I never knew why Sundays, but it was always the only day I ever saw the thing moving until the first of about sixteen nights where my friends and I crammed into the thing for a joyride. I say crammed in because it was only supposed to seat two people, but there were six of us. We made it work. We were creative.

We would take the thing out to Sweetwater to see just how fast we could drive down the winding country roads before a deer decided to say hello or before we lost the ability to keep the car between the ditches. These were country ditches – there was no run-off space outside the lane, you would simply slide into about a three-foot ravine and, if you kept going like Pepper did in his truck one night, you would land somewhere in the woods after you'd lost much of your dinner on the dashboard of the vehicle. I don't know how we managed to get the Porsche up over 100 the sixteenth and final time we did this, but we did. I'm even more surprised that we didn't end up in one of the ditches, and especially shocked that one of the deer we each met in different cars by the end of high school didn't bother to say hello. I do remember that a few years later, in the midst of a brutal car wreck on Interstate 20, I would think that maybe I used up all the vehicular luck I had while flying down Sweetwater those nights.

CHAPTER 17

The first time my kid called me mom freaked me out a little bit. Don't get me wrong, I was and am proud to be one of their mothers, but I just wasn't ready for that term to apply to me.

***

My father – the one who raised me, not Mitchell, well, maybe Mitchell too, but I don't know – has not seen the photos from my second wedding. This is not because they are not publicly available. They are, in fact, on social media. This is not because he cannot see now that he is approaching a ninth decade on the planet. He sees well enough. This is not because I have any intention of keeping them from him. I don't care even a little bit. This is not even because a smart phone he doesn't understand is the only source of internet at my parents' house. My mom has seen them and could easily show him. Nope, he has not seen the photos from my second wedding because my mom is fairly certain he could not handle seeing me in a wedding dress celebrating the day I became a wife – on the marriage contract – and partner – in practice – with my spouse.

I honestly thought my mom might be a little paranoid about this at first. On the one hand, she has a point. He was sure I would ruin my first wedding by wearing a black shirt, as I may have mentioned, so we know he associates clothing with marital success. On the other hand, I've never been all that shy about being who I am, and I am certain he knows – I mean, I've told him myself – about me even though he does a hell of a job never giving any hints that he knows or thinks about it in conversations. I was pretty sure my mom was being paranoid. I thought he would react like her – I don't get it, but I love you – because over the years, they've kind of come around on some things – including voting for a Democrat at least twice that I know of – that seemed impossible when I was a child. I thought she was being paranoid, but only until a potential preview of his reaction emerged in normal conversation one day.

I was sitting and chatting with my mom and two of my – I'm not sure, but I think – cousins who I barely know and don't remember all that well. I was at the end of my teens or maybe in my early twenties the last time I saw them, but in my thirties, they are basically strangers to me. Anyhow, we were catching up – the way strangers do, over small talk – in the living room of my childhood home when I noted the fact that legally I'm a wife. I said this in passing because, for me, it is simply the truth. My spouse and I signed the contract – which had spaces for husband and wife – the way that felt right for us. Well, though he wasn't speaking or otherwise involved in the conversation, my dad was sitting in the room. He exclaimed in surprise, shook his head, muttered something that I did not catch, and left the room for the rest of the night after I said this. Maybe my mom called this one right on the nail, I thought at the time. I was sure the next night when, during a random dinner with my family on one of the rare nights I'm ever visiting my hometown, he brought up the topic and spent a lot of time asking questions about it until again he got up, muttered something I didn't catch, and then disappeared for the rest of the night. My wedding photos are beautiful, but maybe mom is right that if she showed him how to see them, he might no longer be with us.

***

I was fourteen the first time I ever spent any time living alone. I did not run away from home or otherwise move out officially, but I found a dwelling that, for some reason, felt fitting, and I would sneak out of my home at night – sometimes after spending the whole day in my new dwelling – to sleep in the space. This worked out well until the deer that owned and maybe constructed the hut in the woods showed up one night.

People react to loneliness a lot of different ways from what I've seen. Some people respond to feeling isolated by always seeking some kind of company. Some people react to the same isolation by diving into and embracing it in their lives. There are many people who do a wide variety of other things in between these extremes, but I was part of the latter group above. I just embraced isolation. I made lonely my home in some ways. I would take these walks through the woods that would last all day and sometimes all night. I would write in a journal, talk to the scarecrow in the field, and follow the occasional animal to see what its day was like. I just spent a lot of time alone. For some reason, I felt less alone when I was alone. I don't know how that happened, but it was that type of feeling that led me to turn a deer hut I found in the woods into my first independent dwelling. I added a sleeping bag, but otherwise, I left it how it was. I was going for that rustic feeling rich kids who have never been poor love so much. I spent days and nights in that hut just thinking and dreaming. I was sad when it's owner finally came back at a time when I was there. I didn't know – and I never went back to check – if the deer would resume its occupation of the hut, but the dream was broken once another living thing was involved in the equation. I thought a lot about the hut until I found an abandoned house that worked just as well a few months later.

***

The first time I didn't simply pass Atlantic City on a highway in a truck, I spent a couple days there in my late twenties with Mitchell and his husband/partner/spouse – I have heard them use all three words at one point or another – who loved to gamble. They would go there because Mitchell's partner saved money throughout the year to blow at the slot machines. While he did this, Mitchell roamed around Atlantic City making use of the buffets, boardwalk, and other amenities. Since his partner spent a lot of money there, Mitchell got more than a few free gifts along the way and generally had a good time. The year I went with them was the same, but that year included walks and talks with me on the boardwalk.

Rickie, what I'm going to call Mitchell's husband for now, would be up in the casino playing his slot machines. Mitchell and I would grab food, coffee, or whatever before roaming along the boardwalk for hours talking about his life and edited versions of my own life that he seemed to enjoy a bit. I would actually develop a similar pattern a few years later when Nikki became obsessed with playing video poker at casinos. She would play her poker, and I would go roam around, talk to the workers, and otherwise amuse myself. We never did it in Atlantic City, but it was the same idea. Mitchell always surprised me with, what I would call, a very simple version of both his life and the world. He was deeply regretful about many things, and in many ways, he struggled with some serious self-hatred, biphobia, internalized homophobia, and prejudice – some warranted, some extreme – against religion. At the same time, he talked about Texas and his mother who always hated me – though he, for some reason, had trouble believing that part of her existed – in ways that reminded me of a Disney or otherwise fairy tale recording of a life. The combination of his optimism and pessimism – depending on the topic, of course – stuck with me probably more than anything else about our short time hanging out together in New York, Atlantic City, and via email.

***

I have two reoccurring dreams that have been with me for as long as I can remember. I think they might both be memories, but I'm not sure. With one of them, a story my birth mom told me suggests it may well have been a memory, but I'll talk about that one later. The other one, however, I have no clue where it comes from, if it might be a memory, or really anything else about it. I call it my snake dream because I have mostly been terrified of the sight of snakes because of this dream throughout my life. I have made some progress with this fear and may even one day live in the same house as a snake because my life partner loves them, but I still have the dream and still have to remind myself that snakes are generally kind creatures, great pets, and unlikely to hurt a human that didn't first scare or hurt them. It's a process.

The snake dream is always the same. It has never changed. I don't know what that means, but it is one of the reasons I think it could be some kind of memory. I don't know, and I'm not even sure if I want to know to tell you the truth. Anyway, the scene begins in a bedroom. I don't see anything other than the outline of the room. It is dark, but that is all I can tell. I don't know where it is or anything like that. There is a crib in the room. That is what makes me think it is a bedroom. I always see this first, and then I shift perspective. At first, I see the room and the crib. After that, I am, I would guess, a baby because I am something in the crib looking up at what I think is one of those things that people have over cribs that twirls around with multiple objects hanging from it. I watch as a snake, always way too long and thick though different colors for some reason, comes up over the edge of the crib. It stares at me for a few seconds, I don't know how many, and then it enters the crib. It is moving toward me, and I feel fear, pain, and sadness. That's it. That's all I got. I always wake up at the same time, with the same feelings, and I don't know what happens next, if anything, in the dream.

CHAPTER 18

I've never let failure stop me from trying things, but I think maybe it's a good thing that the thing I have thus far failed to accomplish the most times was the ending of my own life.

***

I do not remember my first funeral, but I do remember how it came to pass. I was outside of my aunt's house playing with my own puppy. I sometimes forget that I ever had a puppy because that was the only one I ever had, and I was only a very small child. I was playing with the puppy when my mom told me to come on because it was time to leave. I called for the puppy to come with me, but it did not. Then, I got distracted by something inside the house. When we were backing out of the driveway, the sound of the puppy's, I guess you would call it a, squeal reminded me and my mom we brought the puppy with us that night.

I seem to recall that we did something of the ritual sort to dispose of the puppy, but I never can recall what we did exactly. For a while as a teenager, I thought I imagined the puppy because I had no real memories with it except for its death after I learned I was adopted. I thought the times with the puppy captured in my journals were maybe my own dreams or desires for a pet when I was little. I think maybe a pet made me feel a little less alone, but that might be incorrect. In any case, I found a picture of me with the puppy when I was a teenager. There I was, maybe four or five years old, playing with the thing that looked exactly like the one whose death I could see in my head. We were running together through the field with the scarecrow and the corn in one photo, and I found another photo of me hugging the beast. I wonder what I named that dog.

***

The best thing I ever did for my oldest sister made her hate me for a while. To tell you the truth, it made me hate me for even longer. It was, in some ways, completely evil. It was, in other ways, the kindest and most moral thing I ever did. It was definitely the hardest and most painful lie I ever told. It happened in Aiken, South Carolina. It happened in the middle of my teen years. It happened only a couple years before she died. I can still see it in my head.

I may have mentioned that my oldest sister was the hero of my world as a child. She went to tech school at 16. She had a cool job working in a lab. She drove a Trans Am, had an amazing record collection, and lived in a nicer house than anyone in our family because her and her husband had done well. I worshipped her, and she saved me in so many ways by teaching me to love and embrace all the things about me that were different. She was, well, until she died and became a new person in the stories people told about her life, the black sheep of the family. She was too wild. She was too loud – especially for a girl. She was, as dad would say, "Too smart for her own good." She was one of them "damn liberals" that were so evil in the stories of my youth where adults made sense of the world that made them sad. For me, she was everything.

This was, I think, why having to lie to her that day in the middle of the 90's hurt me so much even though I knew it was the right thing to do. About a year before I lied to her that day, she had left her husband. She was living in a small house in Aiken. She was dealing with the pain of the marriage that no one other than her knew was abusive as all hell with whatever alcohol, drugs, and dangerous adventures with young men she could find. She was hurting herself physically in some of the same ways her husband had before and lashing out at everyone in her life other than me. Throughout that year, we watched her age dramatically. She almost overdosed twice, and she crashed two cars owned by other people. She was dying, slowly, but dying all the same. She even said so. The marriage had finally ended the night the husband beat her so bad that she almost died in a hospital room. He was in therapy and on probation that year. She was falling apart in Aiken, and, as she kept saying, "Trying to dull the feels and beat the shadows."

My parents had been trying to get her to go into therapy at a residential center in Georgia. They had put together the money they could to pay for it. They had many talks with her about it before the day I lied to her. She wouldn't go. She was scared of going to what she called a prison. She didn't want to think about what happened, and she said she knew they would make her think about it. I was the only person, as she put it, "Not trying to lock me up," before the day I lied to her. I don't know if I was right or wrong, but I thought someone needed to be on her side. I was just as scared as everyone else, but I didn't think one more person trying to tell her what to do would do any good. I was not going to do it. I said never each time I was asked to talk to her. I said no. I said no until the day I lied to her.

The day I lied to her I went with my parents to the house in Aiken. They were summoned by the police. My oldest sister had come outside hours before without any clothes screaming about someone trying to kill her. She then proceeded to fire her gun into the house of her neighbor. She didn't hit him, but that probably had more to do with aim and alcohol combinations than anything else. He called the police and told them he was worried that his neighbor would hurt herself or someone else. According to the police, she was back inside the house barricaded in the back room. She was threatening to shoot anyone who came in the room. They called my parents. They said they did this because she had no record other than the one that told them she had been abused. I know all the scientific and medical ways to explain the PTSD break she was experiencing that day now, but at the time, all I knew was that she was going to die that day if someone didn't get the gun away from her.

My parents were going to go into the room, but the officer suggested it should be someone else because she had been cursing them as much as she was cursing everyone else while the cops just outside the room listened. I don't know why or how I did it, but I volunteered to go in, and convinced everyone that I would be the safest option. I didn't know I was right, but I just couldn't believe she would shoot me. When I got inside the room without dying, I told her a lie. I hated doing it, but I couldn't think of anything else to do. I told her that the cops were gone. I told her that Ronald, the guy she was dating at the time who she could easily beat up without much effort, was outside with a car. I told her to trust me, and I would get her out of there. She put down the gun. She hugged me. They cuffed her while she was hugging me. My heart broke when she called me a sick pervert she should have never trusted. It broke again when she screamed that she hated me. I hated me too. Six months later when she came back from the residential treatment center looking like my hero again, I was able to forgive myself as little or as much as I think I'll ever be able to. I have not, however, been able to stop feeling bad about the things she said to me that day, though who knows, maybe one day I'll get over that too.

***

Talking is an art in the south. I don't mean that we take courses to learn how to do the accents that often get northerners to buy us free drinks. I don't mean that we are necessarily aware of the skill it takes to handle and understand southern conversations. I don't even mean that an outsider can interpret our conversations as easily as a given painting. What I mean is that talking in the south is a process that involves very carefully – and without realizing it – learning to have full conversations about nothing and everything all at once.

Having had the opportunity to travel and study people all over the country, I realize more and more when I return to where I'm from on this or that visit that conversations in the south are not the easiest craft to tolerate much less learn. You can go to the average dinner table, and you may notice that the weather, the misadventures of this or that relative nobody gives all that much of a damn about, and that time at that place from so many years ago will be the most common topics. To an outsider, I have learned, this gives the impression that we don't talk about anything. This is incorrect. It is like noticing the color on a painting without catching the reference to an artistic tradition in the brush strokes. It is like enjoying the beat of a Drive-by Truckers song without knowing the reference to this or that southern folk tale mentioned in verse two. It is the surface or the appearance, but not the truth of the moment.

The truth of the matter is that conversations like that tell you the heart of southern experience in my lifetime – endurance. I don't mean the kind of t-shirt you buy at a Charleston tourist trap that says, "the south endures" on it, or some greeting card slogan for people who choose to run when no one is chasing them because they have far too much free time they do not know what to do with, "Endurance, Perseverance, Strength – insert name of gym hoping to make money off your bored white middle-class ass here." No, these are not the kinds of endurance I mean. I mean that most people in south have very little to be happy about beyond the weather, the stories of their families and friends, and the fun things they did once upon a time when they were kids. These are people, aside from the rich few here and there, who work the long shifts, who sweat in the fields, trailers, and housing developments; who wipe the asses and the tables of other people; and who generally have almost nothing in common with anything on television or said in a college classroom. These are people – white, Black, and otherwise – who almost never consider thriving, but rather, live lives built on survival.

There is a reason bands like the Drive-by Truckers and the Carolina Chocolate Drops and writers like Flannery O'Connor and Kiese Laymon have built whole careers talking about sadness, politics, folk tales, and other dark topics in the south – there is an endless supply and almost everyone in the south can relate to these stories in some way, shape or form. On the other side of the political divide in America, this is also the reason things like Fox News and Disney are so popular in the south – they offer a simple, happy story of salvation blended with a vision of the world that is just as sad, unfair, and fucked up as southerners already know it is. This is also the reason churches are so powerful in the region – when you have nothing but hope, hope gets all the money you can possibly spare. Conversations in the south are an art form because people in the south – to varying degrees – have to find a way to communicate with each other without dwelling on just how bad things often are. This is even more true for people of color and queer people in the south. When disaster is the view out the front window, you find a way to talk about anything other than real life. You find a way to celebrate *during* the hurricane, drought, or other calamity.

This is also why so many southern homes almost never turn off the television. Television provides a version of America that so many of the people in the south want to believe exists and maybe even exists for them someday. It also provides endless depictions – from fearmongering politicians to endless murder mystery shows – of just how horrible the world is that allow the people watching these shows to feel a little, just a little is all it takes, better. This is also why the fearmongering works so well, especially for the whites. Southerners have two options for the most part – believe that they have no chance because the world is just that fucked up or believe that the world is only that fucked up because "insert group not like them here" did it. It is much easier to believe in the latter because the former could destroy what little hope you have just like an honest conversation about your daily life over dinner could. This is also why the activist or politician or preacher who best describes a potential source of hope tends to win southern support – within or between different racial, class, gender, and sexual groups in the south – better than anyone else no matter what facts or concrete proposals they have. Hope is what brings them to the churches, and it is the same thing that brings them out to support anything else.

Let me explain the dinner conversation pattern noted above. When you live for the next check and the next world that might be better, here is what those conversation topics really are. Discussion of the weather translates into celebration of the one good thing about living in the region the same way others may talk about a kid's college admittance, a company's success, or any other positive aspect of their lives. It is reminding each other that it is not all bad in this life. Discussion of the misadventures of the random person or on the local news that night is a reminder that at least "we" – whatever family we is at that dinner table – are not "that" bad the same way others put down this or that play they saw, concert they went to, or college they don't like. It is the other side of the insult known far and wide as "well, bless your heart" wherein a family feels better about their lives by sharing the latest fuck up of someone else. Finally, discussion of the time that person did that thing at that place is a reminder that there were good times, that good times will happen alongside the bad ones, and that – especially when rare – good times should be celebrated. It is an attempt to maintain hope in the face of mortgage payments, prescription drug costs, and other things that threaten to destroy you every single day. In the case of southern people of color and queer people in the south, it is a reminder that there are exceptions and possibilities beyond the endless racism, colorism, heterosexism, monosexism, and cissexism – not to mention even higher levels of poverty – sprinkled throughout American existence as a member of these groups.

Talking is an art in the south, and like any good artistic tradition, the truth of the matter exists just as much in what is not said or shown as in what is.

***

My birth mother died almost three years after we met for the first time since I was a baby or toddler, I'm not sure what the cut off between the two is. It was 2014. She was dying from the cancer the whole time we knew each other as adults. I was living in Florida during the same time period. We had some good times together. I got the call, drove to my life partner's house for comfort, and hit the road west to go to the funeral. It was the 39th of my life to date.

I still don't know if my mother's family liked me at all. One of them, her sister, seems to care about me in her own way, but we have nothing in common. One of them, her niece and her sister's daughter, is a fundamentalist Christian who considers everything about me an abomination whether or not she applies that to me specifically and personally. The rest of them are kind of random working and middle and lower class – depending on which one we're talking about – Texans who remind me a lot of the television show *King of the Hill*, but they don't like that comparison. Not surprisingly, I felt out of place and almost entirely unwanted at my mother's funeral. I went anyway. I even stayed longer than I planned simply because my presence seemed to make everyone else uncomfortable. Without her around, I noticed, they had much more trouble talking to me or acting like they cared about me. On the bright side, this contrast suggested to me that they did care for her deeply. I like that. I even like them.

For the first time in my life, my mother's funeral gave me the ability to at least consider the possibility of supernatural powers. This may sound funny but hear me out. My mom, Carly if you recall, did not believe in a Christian god necessarily, but did believe in a higher power. There was a Christian recruitment sermon at her funeral I know she would have hated – she told me as much ahead of time – and her remains were consecrated and put in one of those little cabinets that mausoleums make so much money off of throughout the nation. She didn't want this either and said more than once she thought it was stupid that people did that. She wanted to be cremated and then scattered in nature. She didn't get that wish from her family, if she ever told them, but luckily, some grave robbers – and this is why I wonder if there are supernatural forces now because I could see this happening at her (after life) request – took care of it. The mausoleum was robbed a couple months after her funeral, and hers were among the remains – and of the course the urns that could be sold for money – missing. I'm sure the funeral directors did their best to say what they later found were really her ashes, but I doubt it. Rather, I bet her ashes went floating through some section of woods just like she wanted. I like that too.

CHAPTER 19

Best I can tell, the secret to emotions is to carefully pick where the story begins and ends. If you know when to say cut or roll the credits, every part of your life can have a happy ending. I don't know if this is a useful bit of information or not.

***

I think people who never live there for long portions of time misunderstand the role of ignorance in southern culture. I don't mean ignorance in the sense of the fifteen million comics and comedy routines and Hee Haw skits and political conversations that paint the south as some backwards land of dumb people. I don't mean ignorance in the sense of one who has not learned this or that agreed upon truth at present. I don't mean ignorance in the sense of a blind faith or obedience to this or that leader who swears they have the real answer. No, I don't mean any of these things because these common tropes represent the misunderstanding I've noticed. The misunderstanding is that the south is a place of ignorance, and that education could save the day. I think this is false. The reason I think this is false is because the first part is true – the south is a place of ignorance – but the second part is an outsider fantasy – that education can save the day. The reason is because the ignorance dancing hand-in-hand with endurance throughout the south is not about a lack of knowledge, but rather a redefinition of knowledge.

You have to understand that most people in the south do actually know at least as much factual information as people in other parts of the country from what I've seen. They are not any more or less educated than people in Illinois, California, New York, or anywhere else once you step beyond the stereotypes of the media. The problem is not a lack of information, but rather, what the information means. Information in the south is always up for debate. Feelings rule. Faith rules. Family rules. Racism often rules, sexism as well and homo and bi and trans phobia for that matter. Traditions, even if everyone knows the traditions are bullshit, rule. It is not that southerners don't know the "facts" agreed to by other people, but rather, that they do not choose to agree with the "facts," and instead work around them as much as they can. It is not ignorance in a pure sense (i.e., we don't know), but rather ignorance as a well-developed craft for maintaining what little control they can in the face of difficult and embarrassing contexts (i.e., we do not care what we do or don't know). It is not the person who is ugly but does not know they are ugly, but rather, it is the person who knows they are ugly but works hard to convince themselves this is not important in their case no matter what they may think when no one is around.

This is why I think ignorance and knowledge and belief in the south is so widely misunderstood. People tend to think of these things as passive – I am ignorant until I am exposed to more information on the subject, for example. In the south, however, ignorance is active – it is a craft, a specialized set of skills handed down through families, churches, and schools, a method if you will. This is why, I think, the never-ending onslaught of education campaigns about this or that issue have very little impact on the south. The assumption is that if the people know better, they will live differently. The problem is the people often already know better but choose to live against that information because living differently would require even less control than they already have and more changes than they are willing to make without some concrete payoff. I've had illiterate old people on porches explain, for example, complex intricacies of political economy just as well as Ph.D. colleagues of mine, but the difference is they do not care about these things and see no reason why they should whereas my Ph.D. colleagues – who have had the privilege of an education and paid opportunities – assume that anyone who knew about such things would automatically care. I think this is why it is comfortable for outsiders to talk about ignorance when, in reality, change in the south might more likely begin with a serious discussion about apathy maintained through active ignorance in the face of a world that seems to be against one at every turn and where one's rituals are all they have left to cling to – no matter what the facts say.

***

I think the best Neko Case song is called "Things that scare me." This is not an objective statement in any way. There are likely many arguments that could be made about many songs in Neko's tremendous catalogue. This is not even my favorite song by her. At the same time, and ever since I heard this song for the first time in 2004, I think it is her best work because I feel like we would all be better off if we seriously and intentionally considered the things that scare us for one or a million reasons. In my case, the list is rather short and long at the same time considering everything good, bad, and otherwise I have seen so far.

I am afraid of haircuts, dentists, snakes, love, missing people, emotions, people who appear to be both white and male, baseball bats, the words fag and tranny, woods of various types, and many other things. These are probably the important ones both because my reaction to these things is so automatic that I never have time to think first, and because each one is tied to pieces of me – or the various versions of me that have existed and exist now – that I have lost and gained in painful ways over the years. The reaction to each is visceral – it's beyond the level of thought. These reactions seem the most natural and unnatural thing in the world at the same time. I always think about these reactions, but only after the fact. Sometimes I'm impressed by myself, and other times I'm ashamed, but I always feel like the reactions were as much, if not more, honest than in any other incidents or events that occur in my life. I don't know what that means, or what it says about me, or what it says about fear.

***

I was five years old the first time I remember my gender causing trouble for others. I was on the way to church on a Sunday morning. I always went to church with my mother because I was given no choice. We would meet my older-but-not-oldest sister there. I would go to Sunday school with children my age, and my mother and sister would do the same. We would then, my mother and I, sit together during an always boring service. We would sit in the balcony. My sister did not sit with us. She was in the choir. It was the same routine every Sunday for most of the early years of my life, but one day in the car on the way to the church stands out as my introduction to gender policing or the ways others try to make people fit into whatever religious notion of "your gender should be this or else."

We were driving through our neighborhood listening to the radio. We always listened to the Sunday morning country music countdown because it was music mom liked, and because music was rarely tolerated all that well in my dad's house. He liked a couple artists, but for the most part, he saw music as noise more than anything else and was quick to scream and otherwise throw a tantrum when it was playing somewhere in the house. Headphones were very important in that house. We were driving through our neighborhood when a Reba McEntire song started playing on the radio. I loved Reba even then, and so did mom. I knew all the songs. Mom knew most of them too. Mom would rarely sing along, but I would. I always did, and even love singing along to songs now as much as I did as a kid. I was one of those kids with the hairbrush and the private concert in my bedroom for much of my young life, though usually with headphones, of course.

I was singing along to Reba. I don't remember which song, but that hardly seems important to the story. I was singing along like I always did when my mom turned the radio off. I was more than a little annoyed then, as I am now, when anyone turned off a song that I was listening to. Interestingly, one of the first clues I had that my life partner was a different kind of emotional experience for me was when I noticed that they do this all the damn time without it ever annoying me. I'm still not sure how they manage that since with everyone else I have ever met, this type of action makes me want to – and at times, consider doing so – cut their hands off. When mom did it that day, she turned to me and said, "You should not be singing in such a high voice, people will think you're odd if you sound like that." I responded with the knowledge that I was singing in the same tone that Reba used. "Reba can do that because she's a woman, you should not do that, try to sing more like George Strait or Aaron Tippin." I didn't understand the difference then, and I barely get it on an intellectual level the way any non-believer can kind of grasp the rituals and rules of someone else's faith tradition now, but I complied – only while she was around – for the next few years.

***

I paid for my first abortion when I was 15 years old. I was working at a Burger King. I was making minimum wage. I was in love with a co-worker whose dark skin and yellow car left me wondering what he tasted like in the dark. My friend was pregnant. I had nothing to do with that. She wanted nothing to do with that. She was not working at Burger King.

I was recruited to pay for the abortion because she could not afford one, and the person who provided the sperm donation was nowhere to be found. She told me about the situation over illegal non-tobacco cigarettes we smoked behind the Burger King. She was working at the Huddle House across the street, making even less money than I was. We had to do some research since the only thing we knew about abortion at the time was that our separate though similar churches hated them and the characters on *90210* had mentioned them once or twice in episodes. Neither of us were from the types of families that had the internet in the 1990's, and thus we went to the local library one day before either of our work shifts, but after school. That first day all we really accomplished was figuring how to use the internet to an extent. It was a process. We went back four more times before figuring out what to do.

I took her to the clinic we found, and she handled, as she put it, the "trash disposal" on a Saturday afternoon when we were both off work. The first thing she said after being quiet for a couple hours after the event was that, especially considering all the shit on the internet and in churches, it was a bit anti-climactic. She expected something more difficult or emotional or something like that. She expected to want this or that or something else related to it. All she wanted was some frozen yogurt. I was surprised by her reaction, but quite used to the ways churches and media ramped up expectations that never quite fit reality. I also figured the reaction might be similar or very different for other people facing the same experience and have seen varied reactions since from different people in the same situation. I got a yogurt with some peanut butter in it. She got sprinkles. We spent the evening behind the Burger King sitting beside empty yogurt containers smoking illegal non-tobacco cigarettes. It was the first of the six abortions I have purchased in my life to date.

CHAPTER 20

There are scars all over my body that are visible to others. There are many more scars within my body and mind that no one can see without a tour guide.

***

I woke up in a very dirty hotel room in Las Vegas in 2011. It was summer. I was many miles from my home. Nikki had just moved out. My birth mother had paid for the hotel room. I was hungover. I had just slept with two people the night before. One was a local man I never saw again. The other was a woman I would see a few more times. I was supposed to be networking at an academic conference. I was actually contemplating suicide. I had not told anyone this. My birth mother did not know I found a gun I could buy easily at a pawn shop when I got into town. Nikki did not know she might have seen me for the last time. I wasn't close to anyone else in my life at that point except a woman named Michelle I barely knew but felt close to every time we hung out at academic conferences.

I spent the day before with Michelle. I spent the night before getting too drunk not to sleep with two strangers at different points. I spent an hour in a casino on the corner enjoying all the sounds after my first bump of cocaine in years. It would be my last, at least so far, though at the time, I meant that in a different way. I don't have anything profound to say about that weekend. I was simply in pain. Years before, I had gotten used to what felt like a numbness that I think came from burying so many good people who I thought were better than me, but something about my time with Nikki and meeting my birth mom ripped that numbness away from me. I felt the loss again, like I did when I was younger and using cocaine and alcohol much more than a doctor would advise, and I wanted to stop feeling it. This was complicated by pain in my face due to the lingering effects of a bigot with a baseball bat who rearranged my mouth one day on a sidewalk during that same prior period of my life. My face hurt so much, and the rest of me followed suit. I wanted it to stop.

I came to Las Vegas because there was a conference there, and that would make it a travel destination that no one would think twice about. I also came because my birth mother and birth father had come there when they were in their early twenties, and I had thus far managed to visit everywhere they had been together and separately on my own as if I was taking a tour of their lives. I came to Las Vegas with three options. I could go back to graduate school and finish my degree. I could then move on to life as a Ph.D. – whatever that meant – and try again to not end up suicidal in a random hotel room. It was possible this time could be different, I thought, but I wasn't hopeful. I could go anywhere from Las Vegas – I brought what I needed to keep, and my lease would be up soon – and just disappear like I tried to do so many times on so many trucker drives north in my early twenties. This time I had some more lessons from life and a couple degrees, so maybe I could build a new life that way. Finally, and what seemed the most appropriate thing to do as I sat there in my own vomit on the floor of that hotel room that morning, I could just give up and say goodbye.

I don't have any real insight to share here, as I noted above, because I don't know why I didn't die that weekend. It wasn't because something amazing happened that saved me the way that so often occurs at the end of movies. It wasn't that I was suddenly in less pain, though the pain would lessen within the next year, well, the physical pain would, the other stuff would take much longer. It wasn't that I felt necessarily pulled in any way to stay alive. I mean, I had just met a kid named Gibbard that I knew needed help and a role model, but overly worrying about what other people might need had never been something I cared for much. I don't know why or how I got off the floor that morning. I don't know why or how I showed up for the job interview I had scheduled at the conference fully dressed in just as professional attire as anyone else. I don't know why or how I made it out of Las Vegas, and maybe I never will.

***

The worst thing Ernie ever did was fall in love with me back when I was 23. I don't know this for sure, mind you, but I know this was the worst thing he ever did that I knew about.

The problem in this case was that Ernie made a cardinal mistake that many other people in my life have made, and only a few, so far, have not lived to regret at least somewhat. This mistake was the assumption that I was capable of loving someone. Again, in three cases, I have done this, maybe even four cases I think now, but it is incredibly rare if you do the math and set the equation between people I have met, or even played with intimately, versus people I have fallen in some kind of deep emotional bond like thing with. Ernie may have been one of the most wonderful people I ever met, and I did have lots of fun with him. The problem was that Ernie wanted more than I could offer and was too invested to accept this fact until it was far too late to do so without hurting him tremendously. Letting himself love me – for Ernie, this was, according to him as he stormed out of the house after he caught me in bed with someone else, the worst thing he ever did. I never saw him again after that. I was gone – with my stuff, of course – from his house before he returned, I would guess, at some point.

***

When I was a teenager, some friends and I had a terrible rule. We agreed that if it was funny, you couldn't get mad. The "it" here referred to pretty much any kind of prank or joke, and the "funny" referred to the ability of anyone in the group to find it funny. This was not the best recipe for kindness or sensitivity, but it opened the door to many pranks.

While we came up with many pranks during our teen years, my favorite one involved an abandoned church in the middle of the woods halfway down Sweetwater Road. You could not find this church by accident. It was seven miles down a winding dirt road in the woods. There was no electricity nearby. There were only a few abandoned houses spread out over the area at various points in the – for lack of a better phrase – road. It was the epitome of isolated. There were also stories about the place. It was rumored to be the sight of a long-ago massacre, which naturally meant it was haunted. One of the nearby abandoned houses was said to have belonged to an old man who went crazy in the 1800's and butchered hundreds of other people. He was said to roam the woods near the place. No one ever seemed to ask where he found hundreds of people to butcher in the middle of the woods. There was also the story of a baby who was drowned in a creek nearby, just down the hill from the church, that continued to haunt the area. I doubt any of this was even close to realistic or even based in truth, but it was fun to think about the stories and use them to scare people.

When I was in high school, some friends and I figured out the perfect prank for this place. A friend of mine, we'll call him Freddy, had a Mustang, and it was one of those cars that are so common now where you can lower the back seat to make more storage space. We had another friend who I'll call George who could fit in the trunk. We practiced for a while and figured out George could climb through the backseat into the front of the car with enough time. This was the crux of the prank. We would take other people, usually younger folk from school, out to the "haunted church" in the middle of the night. I was in the passenger seat ready to educate the kids about the church after we got there. Freddy was driving and acting a little scared for dramatic effect. George was hidden in the trunk without the knowledge of whoever our passengers – or targets – were that night. When we got to the church, we parked about 200 yards from the building, and Freddy left the headlights on. This was crucial because it meant that from the church all we – or our guests – could see was the headlights if they happened to look back at the car.

The prank played out in the following ways. First, we would go in the church with our guests – it was just a one room thing falling apart – and talk to them about the wood, the church, and the stories. Second, we would all hear the car start and Freddy and I would react with surprise while the guests reacted in fear. At this point, sometimes we had another friend in the woods who would make noise around us, sometimes we did not. In any case, to further sell the point, Freddy would pull out his keys, carefully having taken the battery out of the little remote on the way into the church and shake them trying to control the car while running toward it. When he got halfway to the car, the third phase began. George would squeal the tires and kick up mud and dirt as he backed the car onto the dirt road and took off down the hill. Freddy would chase the thing – usually being accompanied by one or both of our guests. More slowly, I would, in the right amount of time, catch up with him. He would be standing in the dirt road with his keys cursing and staring down the hill. The car would be stopped on the bridge over the creek at the bottom of the hill with only the lights visible in the darkness.

Without anything else to do, we would agree to walk to the car. When we got to the car, phase four of the prank would kick into gear. There was a way to crank a Mustang at the time without actually cranking it up. Freddy figured this out when his brother tricked him into thinking the car was broken when it was not by doing the same thing. While our guests, every damn time without instruction, stood around the car with me, Freddy would get in the car and try to start it – wink, wink. It wouldn't start, and this was part of the dead baby legend. After three tries, I don't know why we chose that number, George would start playing a CD we made of baby sounds from his position hiding under the bridge. The sounds would spill throughout the night, and we would watch our guests – or targets – lose their damn minds for about fifteen minutes – that was as long as we could ever keep from laughing.

***

The earliest prank I ever pulled involved the scarecrow in the field near my house. One day, I don't know why, I wanted to know what the world looked like through its eyes. I might have been 7 or 8 years old at the most, and I was fairly tiny, so I climbed up the wooden post it lived on and slid the clothes off the hay body. I then pulled down the hay body, put on the clothes, and climbed back up to the top of the post. I stayed there for a few hours, but after about an hour, my day in the life of a scarecrow changed from an observational to a humorous endeavor.

This happened completely by accident. Some kids that were even younger than me came by after I had been up there for about an hour enjoying the view. They were not bothering me, but I wondered if they had noticed me at all. I started just saying random things, like, "When the sun speaks, the tigers hear, and when the tigers speak, the world listens," stupid shit. The kids didn't know where the voice was coming from, I apparently did a good job of passing as a scarecrow, thank you very much. It may have been because of the darkness that day rather than my own talent, but I'm taking credit anyway. They ran off screaming and crying. I enjoyed this. It was fun and kind of fascinating to my young mind. I did it again with three more groups of kids before it got late enough that I didn't expect any more kids and I thought I would be in trouble if I didn't get home soon.

CHAPTER 21

Maybe it is a product of where I was raised, but the other day I realized that I have had nineteen different friends – to various degrees of closeness, mind you – named Bob in my life, and every single one of them had some form of a drinking problem at some point.

***

Most of my dad's family lived in Augusta when I was a child. This was the same place my father was born and raised long before raising me across the river in South Carolina. I don't remember much about this family, but I do somewhat recall visiting some of their homes. There was one, in particular, that I enjoyed because it was full of all kinds of machines that I would take apart and play with during family visits. There were gumball machines, old arcade machines, machines that were some type of crank I never figured out, and machines that I never could identify in any way. It was cluttered and dirty, and there was some relative named Bob that was either living in the house somewhere or maybe around the corner, I don't really remember. What I do remember is how much fun the machines were.

My favorite out of the whole bunch was my dad's sister, we'll call her Louise. Louise passed away when I was a teenager, but every time I saw her alive, she was mad at some person, place or thing. The woman could go on for an hour about how much she hated this or that town. I enjoyed these rants. I especially enjoyed when she would get pissed off at my dad and yell at him for – best I could tell – no reason. She seemed to be the only person he was ever afraid of, and since I was often afraid of him, I liked that. I don't think I ever saw her sober, but I'm not sure if she was ever all that drunk. One of her relatives, I'm not sure which one, said she kind of lived in a buzz. She would get tipsy and yell at things – it seemed like an interesting life. It was especially fun because she was married to one of the quietest people I ever met, and he just happened to have impeccable manners. I always enjoyed the contrast between the two of them – she was a tornado, and he was the calm before it.

The only other thing I ever really remember about my dad's family is that his own father was very disappointed in him. The family had apparently done fairly well, in working class white southerner terms, at some point during Jim Crow times, but his father believed my dad's meat cutting occupation was a bit of a step down for the family. I heard him say this a couple times in a couple ways. We would be at the house he lived in on Greene Street, which doesn't exist anymore, and he would be about as grouchy and confrontational as my dad usually is. I would listen to them maybe argue or maybe talk for a while before going to the back of the house to talk to the old guys. The old guys were the people who rented rooms in the back of the house. They would be sitting outside most days playing checkers, smoking cigarettes, and complaining about the economy. I'm not sure if any of them ever did anything for a living, but they seemed to be at the house, out back laughing and telling stories, every time I ever went there.

***

The most important Bob I ever knew was a good friend of mine in high school. He was about the opposite of cool and confident, and I'm pretty sure this was part of what I liked about him. He was desperately interested in fitting in, and I was amused by the fact that he had maybe the only more difficult daddy than mine. He lived in one part of town. I lived in another. He loved Waffle House. I liked to read there. We met over my coffee and his sweet tea and spent the next few years roaming around towns and woods together.

Throughout the 1990's, this Bob and I would often be found in this or that Waffle House cutting up with the workers. His dad basically lived in these places, and this was only one of the first ways he became more and more like his dad over time. He was interested in computers, and many of my earliest lessons with those machines came at his house while he drank Mountain Dew and talked about one day finding him a girl. He was mostly important to me because he may have been the most purely nice person I ever met, and I watched over the course of a decade as that quality was beaten out of him by angry kids, an even angrier father, factory work, alcohol, and finally working in a grocery store in the middle of the night. It was an amazing transformation. He was the kind of person who would give you the shirt off his back, but he became the kind of person who hated everything. He was the kind of person who would drive for hours to do a random acquaintance a favor, but he became the kind of person who never smiled at all. He was the kind of person everyone said we should be, but everything in our town beat all the kindness out of him little by little.

＊

Sometimes, you have to do things you don't want to do to get a ride home. Sometimes this involves performing sexual favors for truckers. Sometimes this involves putting up some cash for gas money that will take you farther if you have your own car. Sometimes this means waiting for Tommy to fuck Tasha or the other way around in a rusty trailer on the outskirts of a broken down and abandoned factory town in rural South Carolina. Sometimes this simply means hearing that someone loves you and giving them hugs because that is how they become after a few drinks.

I learned this last example from a guy with three DUI's who also frequented some parties at another guy's house out in the woods. This guy would show up with beer – lots of it – and chill out talking to everyone until his fifth beer. After his fifth beer, he would become a hug machine that moved throughout the party telling everyone he loved them in, sometimes, especially creepy ways. He was a bit older than everybody else at these parties, but if this was something he noticed, I never saw any hint of it. He was technically without a license, but he was always willing to drive anyone home without asking for gas money. He had a blue car. There were always beer bottles all over the thing, and there were also empty packs of smokes everywhere. The damn thing smelled like a dive bar. He did too. This was especially uncomfortable because he would go through the whole, "I love you," thing and have to get a hug or nine before he finally would let you go once you got to your front door. It was cheaper than gas money, but in the end, it was kind of more expensive at the same time.

***

The most important trip I ever took was a road trip in the summer of 2014. I was two years out of graduate school. I was two years into the best job I ever had. I was returning from my birth mother's funeral, but we'll get to that part of the story. My birth mother's funeral was in east Texas where she was born and raised. I had driven there from central Florida with only one stop at my life partner's home. On the way back, I decided to take my time, and visit some places along the route. I needed to think.

My road trip began with a passage through rural parts of east Texas I had only seen on a map. I drove through these areas on my way to my birth father's hometown in Louisiana. I reached that hometown in the first day and spent most of the evening taking pictures of the place. I walked the tiny downtown area reminiscent of my hometown and sat writing in my latest journal for about an hour at the commemorative train station that was no longer in use. I planned to stay the night, but I changed my mind when I remembered another place in Louisiana that I should visit. I fired up a Lucinda Williams album on my iPod and hit the road. I drove through rural – somewhat northern – Louisiana heading east and south until I landed in Slidell. I stayed the night at a cheap hotel like the one I worked at in college. I chose the hotel because social media taught me Gillingham's mom worked there. We didn't talk. She recognized me. I recognized her. Her co-worker checked me in that night. We didn't talk. She stared at me as if she was meeting the devil. I stared right back at her. We didn't talk.

I slept restlessly in the hotel that night. It was cold. It was dirty. It was loud. I was propositioned each time I went outside for a smoke. It was almost exactly like the one I used to work at. It was almost exactly like one Gillingham and I stayed in a long time ago as young kids in love who never considered that only one of them would live long enough to think about how young we were then. I don't really know how, but I put him to rest that night. I still miss him. I still love him. Hell, I think in some ways, my life partner even loves him through me. I still think about him. I still don't think we would have lasted even if his life would have lasted longer. I still wonder if there is a space beyond this life where he might hear this. I still hope I haven't let him down too much. I don't think any of these things will ever change, but how they feel changed that night. For lack of a better phrase, I think I let him go that night, and in so doing, I let myself out of an unseen box for the first time in years that night. I saw his mom again when I checked out right after sunrise. We didn't talk. I left for Mississippi.

Mississippi had little personal relevance for me, but I felt drawn there that summer. It was the site of my life partner's birth. It was the title of my favorite Bob Dylan song. It was the site of my new (at the time) favorite novel, *Long Division*, and so many Grisham novels. It was the site of a job I wanted that didn't work out. That was it. I had no real connection to the place, and yet, I felt like I needed to stop in that state. I don't know how to explain this feeling, but I followed it. I drove up the gulf coast until a hotel standing all by itself in a small town called Long Beach seemed to speak to me. I stopped the car. I checked into the hotel. I got a nice room high up in the building with a nice view of the gulf. I didn't know why I was there, but that didn't seem important because it just felt right. I spent the next few days roaming around Long Beach. I got fairly decent sea food at a restaurant that was also a pier, and I spent hours writing in my journal at a bank that had been converted into a coffeehouse. I spent some afternoon time at a used bookstore that looked far larger than I would have expected in a town that small.

I felt a sense of freedom I had lost sight of over the years. I don't know how to explain it, but I felt like it was time to move forward with my life. I felt like it was okay that my life partner was something I was becoming certain I did not want to live without and eclipsing what I had with Gillingham at the same time. I felt like it was okay that I was building an actual friendship with someone else who I actually wanted to know me in all my many iterations. I walked on the beach at night and felt like I was closing the prior chapter of my life. I was 33 years old, and it seemed like the next chapter was beginning if I could just locate the courage not to run away from it. I left Mississippi a few days later convinced I possessed the necessary courage, and in so doing, began a new phase in my life that, to date, is rather enjoyable.

CHAPTER 22

When I'm happy, I send people pictures of turtles. When I'm up to no good, I send people pictures of monkeys. When I'm sad, I don't deal with people.

***

There was a movie called *The Cowboy Way* that came out sometime during my teen years. I saw it at a friend's house. I watched it with two friends, actually. The movie was not very good, nor all that memorable. For some reason, this didn't stop my friends and I from calling each other Sonny, Pepper, and Nacho after characters in the film. We did this so much that other people started calling us these names. I don't remember much about the guy named Nacho, but Pepper and I accidentally became roommates a few years later.

I say accidentally because none of it was planned. I say accidentally also because nothing was ever official – there was no lease, there was no deposit, and there was no mail sent to the trailer with our names on it. In fact, there was no furniture now that I think of it. The trailer was one another friend rented out in the middle of nowhere. It was a classic three-bedroom piece of shit on blocks. It was on a paved road that became dirt about block further from where we lived. It was where we shut off the power to scare people on Y2K, and it was where we used milk crates for coffee tables, chairs, and whatever else we needed. We had one plate and two spoons. We had a Waffle House twenty minutes away down the dirt road. We had water and power and a television with a bunny-ears antenna. The other friend was fresh from a divorce after fifteen years of marriage and dating Pepper's cousin. His room had a bed. The bed was a rental or rent-to-own I should say. He worked at the train yards. Pepper did too. I didn't do much of anything.

We were living in this space when Pepper fell pretty far behind on his truck payments. This was partially my fault. I needed cocaine and professional "dates." Pepper liked cocaine and whores.

137

We spent two paychecks of his in a row on cocaine. We gave some of it to "dates" for obvious reasons. I was fighting with my boyfriend. Pepper never knew I had boyfriends. Our other friend worked a lot and yelled about the beer bottles everywhere whenever he came home to the trailer. Most of the bottles were his. We didn't share our cocaine with him. We said this was because of the yelling, but it really wasn't. Pepper's truck got put on one of them lists that are given out to repo men. We knew a guy who knew the big repo man in the area. I dated his son Jamal at one point, but that's another story. The big repo man told the guy we knew when Pepper's truck got added. Pepper didn't have money. I wasn't sharing mine. I told him I didn't have any. Our other friend wasn't around. Pepper came up with a solution. He would take the stick shift out of his truck every night before bed so it could not be cranked up by a repo man. We learned this trick from Jamal. Pepper later became a cop and had seven kids with three women. We lost touch at some point.

***

I don't remember if it was Karen or Felice who taught me about cocaine. By taught, I mean one of them shared some with me at the end of the 1990's. By the end of the 1990's, I think I mean around 1998 or 1999. It was the end of high school. I met them hanging out with one of the Bob's at a Waffle House. They were both in their 20's. They were both dating people they hated. They were both funny. They both did cocaine for, as one of them but I'm not sure which one put it, "A little spice." They were both between colleges. I sat between them in a booth a lot of nights.

I didn't have what I would call a habit until a few years later, but this was my first taste. I had smoked a bit off and on as a teen, and I drank when other people were just to have something to do, but this was the ticket. I also tried all the goodies – weed, x, acid, etc. – but nothing really got me going the way cocaine did. It was good shit. It was bad shit. It felt great. It felt terrible. It was just inconsistent enough to appeal to me. There were more than a few times later in my life when I crossed state lines with enough to begin discussing federal levels, but at this point, I was more of a baby experimenting with Karen or Felice. You know what, maybe I did cocaine with both of them and that's why I can never remember which one it was.

***

As funny as it sounds to me now, I was completely in love with the New Kids on the Block for a little while in the 1980's. It wasn't the music. I thought that was crap, mostly. It wasn't the outfits. Theirs were as silly as everyone else's in the 1980's / the Target store collection circa 2014. It was the boys themselves – they were so damn cute.

At the time, there were a bunch of teen magazines like there are now. We didn't have the internet and I didn't have cable, but we had radio countdown shows and television countdown shows that would come on each week. I collected pictures of the New Kids that I pasted in every spare spot on my bedroom walls. I would stare at them and dream of the day Joey would marry me and take me away from South Carolina. Like so many of the other girls in school, I was so sure that Jordan was sexier, but Joey was more the marriage type of guy for me. I remember almost participating in many of these debates on the playground. Obviously, some people liked Donnie the most, but I found him kind of creepy even before his acting career. I would sing Joey's parts in the songs into my hairbrush in a whisper so as not to annoy my dad. I enacted the way Joey would propose to me so many times in that little room. The bastard never showed.

***

One of the most, in my opinion, fascinating things that ever happened to me occurred in my 30th year on the planet. I was a graduate student. I was well educated. I was hanging out with my birth mother in Disney. I was talking to her about her family history. My birth father, indirectly deciding where I went to graduate school, but that's a story for another time, had told me some things that turned out to be false. At the same time, my birth mother told me some things that surprised me. It turned out that while I was labeled legally white by my adoptive parents after they collected me from Texas, my actual genetic makeup was much more complicated.

I remembered different times in my life when people yelled slurs often directed at Hispanic people at me. I remembered the time an old white guy asked me what part of Mexico I was from. I remembered the date in high school that said she always wanted to be with a Latin lover. I remembered many more examples, and I even have a couple from earlier this year. All of these things confused me. I figured that at some points and in some settings where the light was done a certain way, maybe I looked somewhat Hispanic. I figured that it had something to do with sunlight and skin tone because it always happened – still does – when I was spending more time outside than usual and more often than not, it happened in the summer. This sounded fine to me. I didn't care. I still don't care. What my mom told me was that there were apparently, if you went back just a little, reasons for these experiences. I found out similar information through genetic testing, but that was boring. Having been raised white and being seen as white most of the time, this was a rather fascinating experience that I still don't know how to make sense of in any real way.

CHAPTER 23

If I had to pick one, I think MAD Cat from Inspector Gadget would be my ideal role model.

***

There are expressions that seem to fit my own ancestry and background better than I would like. One of these expressions is "family problem." A family problem, at least in the part of the south I grew up in, refers to a recurring "issue" in a family that no one talks about publicly. This "issue" is often drug, alcohol, or sex related in most cases, and in my case, it is primarily the last one, but the first two come up to make appearances here and there.

From what I can gather, I think it started with my great grandfather – biologically speaking, though I never met him. There are rumors that my grandmother killed him, but the official record says he committed suicide before he reached the age of 50. He was apparently deeply in the bottle and rather abusive by any measure, but the family problem was that he would disappear for days and weeks on end. He may have been in hotels with women or men or both, I have heard, but the general consensus is he was up to no good, and whatever he was doing, it was not staying in place with his family. I don't know if there are others before him, but the pattern of disappearance alongside premature death or injury continued with my grandfather who I apparently look like at times. He was the only one of my great grandmother's who I thought was my grandmother's children to leave the town where they were raised. He left for the west. He left for Louisiana. He left to form a trucking company. He was gone a lot as an adult, rumors abound as to what he was doing as well, and then died before the age of 50 on the side of a road when he got out to check his tires.

My own father, remember Mitchell, stayed at home until his father died, but then he disappeared too. He went to Las Vegas, to Houston, to New Orleans, to New York, and to a few other places before landing most recently in Connecticut. I'm afraid of Connecticut, but that's another story for another time. I know he was playing with boys in ways that our families would not exactly embrace, but to his credit, aside from a couple near misses, he has managed not to die and passed the age of 50 at this point. I am the next link, and well, disappearance is one of the few things I've ever been good at, but what can I say, it's a family problem.

***

I was happy when my baseball career ended. Well, I was in incredible pain, but I was also happy. I wasn't happy because of any animosity toward the game or my teammates or the chance to maybe be one of the few to go college someday. I was fine with these things, and these things helped me keep playing long after the game stopped being fun. No, I was happy because I lost interest in playing around the time I was 12, but since it was something I was good at that was read by my family as something good, I kept playing.

I was better at the game than I think anyone would have predicted. There was something about the geometry of the game that spoke to me and made much of it easy. I played most of my early life, and only stopped when the perfect excuse arose. This perfect excuse was a leg injury due to a poorly implanted base. If you've ever seen the spike on the bottom of those bags, you can guess the kind of pain I was in that day. This injury made running, and at times even walking, quite difficult, and my athletic pursuits – well, those outside of bedrooms and other hidden spaces – died slowly but surely. I was happy for this turn of events, if not the way it happened, because it meant I had more time to read, play music, and sleep around. These hobbies that I was at least halfway decent at were not nearly as prestigious as sports glory, mind you, but I was already much more invested in them than I ever was in baseball.

***

The most important thing that dating ever taught me was that there is no objective truth, reality, or opinion to be found among humans. Let me illustrate this for you.

When I was seeing a guy named Derrick, my gay and lesbian friends were over the moon happy. Derrick was a good guy, they said. Derrick was a perfect match for me, they said. Derrick was an example of what we all wanted, they said. My straight friends, on the other hand, hated Derrick. Derrick was too loud, they said. Derrick was messy and didn't really fit in, they said. I could do better, and I shouldn't settle for Derrick, they said. The few bi friends I had said both of these things to varying degrees, but overall, they just kept saying they wanted me to be happy. It was a contradiction.

After I stopped seeing Derrick, I began seeing a chick (her favorite word) named Cindy. My gay and lesbian friends hated Cindy. Cindy was annoying, they said. Cindy was always trying to outsmart everyone, they said. Cindy and I just didn't fit, they said. I should not settle for Cindy, they said. My straight friends, on the other hand, were in love with Cindy. Cindy was a great girl, they said. Cindy really complemented me, they said. Cindy was exactly the type of partner everyone should have, they said. My bi friends once again said all these things but stuck to the same overall support approach with Cindy they had with Derrick.

Cindy did not last either. I later started dating a non-binary person named Ace. This became even more interesting because my gay friends hated them. They said many of the same things they said about Cindy. My straight friends hated them too and shared the same opinions of my gay friends. My lesbian friends, to my surprise, loved them for the most part, but mostly adopted the we want you to be happy approach of my bi friends. My bi friends remained consistent in their responses, echoing themselves in the other two cases, which was kind of funny considering the fluidity that dominated other aspects of their lives. At this point, I was simply curious, so I started adding other variables into this dating equation. I would date Black men and women and non-binary people and watch the reactions. The bi people stayed the same in these cases, and the others varied. Then, I dated some trans men and other trans women of different races and classes, and again, the bi people stayed the same, but the others varied. I kept doing this for the better part of a couple years, and throughout it all, what I learned was that what constituted a good partner for me in the eyes of others was heavily tied to their own pre-established beliefs about dating.

***

I see things that other people don't see. I'm not talking about my career as an observer of social life here. I'm not talking about the unique standpoint of a white queer, trans person from the south who happens to be adopted and agnostic either. I mean that I actually see things that even I am pretty sure are not really there. I don't know why this happens, but it does.

I was walking down the road in my neighborhood this morning, for example, and without any warning, a group of multi-colored elephants and alligators started dancing across the highway. Now, there were cars coming in both directions that did not suddenly hit these orange, pink, blue, and purple animals. This leads me to believe they weren't really there. This is not an unusual thing for me. For example, I don't generally listen to most people I talk to, and as a result, the phone is uncomfortable for me in most contexts. Rather, I tend to read what people say most of the time. They speak, and words appear over their heads or on their faces like you see in cartoons. I read the words, and sometimes correct the grammar, but I rarely "hear" much of what they say. Instead, I often hear them in other languages I don't know that my brain knows, or I hear a song that reminds me of them playing in the background. I don't know why this happens, but it does.

People also change a lot when I see them. Sometimes their skin will shift colors fourteen or forty times during a conversation, and other times they will just be a color – most often it is purple, yellow, or orange if that matters for your diagnosis – instead of a human body. Sometimes they will take on the shape of whatever they are talking about, and other times I will see what I can only guess is my interpretation of matter forming and dissolving them into different shapes as they speak. It's a little eerie, but also kind of fun. When I was little, I would point these things out to people as they spoke, but I realized quickly that doing so was not the best idea. You would think that people who are able to believe in zombies who die on a cross and come back to save the world could handle my own imagination, but alas, the answer was emphatically no. I had the same issue with scientific types when I first started being around them. You would think that people who believe we can study all manifestations of the world and consciousness would be fascinated to hear of another different one, but alas, the answer was also emphatically no. In the former case, I scared them. In the latter case, I scared them. In both cases, I found their reactions surprising and hilarious at the same time.

CHAPTER 24

My colleague does not want his science class to seem like an art class. I intentionally do what this colleague is trying to avoid because arts tend to be more effective at inspiring critical thought, political action, and emotional responses to the data and the world. I don't know if this matters to you, but I thought I would share it just in case.

***

The biggest lesson I have learned in my time making a living as a scientist is that I am far too honest to be a scientist. I don't mean to suggest that scientists are intentionally dishonest. This is the opposite of what I have seen. Rather, I mean that I have trouble suspending disbelief or having faith in anything, and for the most part, that ability is just as necessary in science as it is in any religion I have encountered so far.

In fact, my experience with religions allowed me to make sense of science much easier than I would have been able to otherwise. The same way that religious people often point to the scripture when you say anything they disagree with, many scientists will ask for a journal article citation when you say anything they disagree with. Neither group ever asks for these sources when you say something they already agree with. The same way many religious people will take a few examples from this scripture or that preacher or that book by someone talking about the scripture and extrapolate that to everyone, much of science involves taking samples of 2000 or 4000 people at most and extrapolating that to everyone. Religious people call this process putting the scripture into the world, and scientists call it generalizability. Where I grew up, people also called it stereotyping. Neither the scientists or the religious people I've met like it if you call it that, but if you point out that in both cases someone is taking less than 1% of the available data (i.e., that one guy they know down at the market) and saying things about the other 99% (other people are like that because that guy in the market is like that), well, then they get really mad.

This is, of course, what I mean about being too honest for either of these traditions. I will simply say that this sample of people said x, and this scripture said y. They don't like that, probably because both are pretending with all their might that they have more control and know more absolutes than is likely possible. I also have trouble with both traditions because while I was growing up in the 80's, 90's and even the 00's and now, people like me did not exist for the most part in the "truth" both groups were so certain of and committed to. I can tell you from experience that if someone tries to sell you a truth that does not include your existence, it is incredibly difficult to see that truth as anything other than a sales job by someone seeking control, power, or something else that has nothing to do with the reality you live in every day. This, of course, is why religions and sciences are forced to change so much over the course of time. Sooner or later, reality does that annoying thing where it doesn't stop existing for the sake of humanly created stories, numbers, or theories.

***

I like the rain a lot. I generally love water in almost any case, but I especially have an affection for the rain. This manifests in different ways and has since I was a kid.

There are two kinds of rain I truly adore. The first is the type of rain that Florida is known for – where the bottom seems to drop out of the sky and a torrential downpour covers the lands for five minutes to fifteen hours on a given day. When this happens, as I have always done since I was a very small child, I sit somewhere outside under a covering of sorts and either write or just watch the water flow while smoking and listening to music. I don't know why, but something about this calmed me as a child, and it still does. I will spend hours just watching the downpour and listening to the sound of the drops – which sometimes sound like bricks in such cases – pound against the roof of whatever covering I am under at the time. There is something wholesome or maybe natural to this type of moment for me that words don't seem to capture well. I hate that part, but I also feel like that somehow makes it even better.

The other kind of rain I love the most is the light, misty kind of rain that often comes before and after a given storm surge. Sometimes there will be weeks where this is happening every night in the states I have lived in, and I crave it. It is the magical space between raining hard enough to be annoying if you have to go to your car, and not raining at all that fills me with energy and desire. I will go out walking for minutes or hours in the mist, and feel it wash over me metaphorically and actually. There is something about this experience that often triggers some of my best ideas and least likely to actually be accomplished plans. Both of these experiences, when triggered, often make me feel more real, or maybe just more stable, than I usually know how to feel in the rest of my life. I think it might have to do with the fluidity of the moisture in the air and against my body, but I'm not sure.

***

My first experience with group sex felt like an out of body experience. It was like I was watching it. It was like I wasn't living it. It was like a movie, but someone else was the director if you wish to know the credits. It was surreal, but also interesting. I think that was it – the experience was, at least the first time, more interesting than it was sexual for me.

I distinctly remembering losing consciousness of what was happening and what I was doing. Instead, I felt like I was reading the event in the novel someone else wrote about the night. There was Donna who never stopped talking except when sexual activities started. She often freaked out girls and guys alike by her complete silence in the bedroom. There was Donny who never seemed all that comfortable during the whole thing but talked about it more than anyone else after the fact. He became a pastor, and I often enjoy remembering that I had an orgy with a pastor. There was Lenore who was the only one of us that had ever had group sex before that night. She was in charge. She was our leader. She was a redhead from Alabama who talked with a fake French accent a lot for some reason I never learned or could have likely understood.

There was Marta who was fresh out of the military and newly discovering her interest in women. She spent almost the entire time tentatively touching the female bodies right before diving into a male body, and then repeating the cycle until the last few minutes when she became entangled with Donna. Other than me, there was finally Sky who was quite fond of being whipped and bitten. They got more than their fair share of both by the end of that night just in case you're curious. We were piled on a king size bed in a motel room in Aiken, South Carolina for this particular event, and I kept wondering if the night clerk that expressed interest in joining us would ever show up. He did not. I don't know if that was his loss or ours.

What I remember most from that night is not the sex, but rather, the interesting ways different bodies could become tangled up together in a limited space. It was like I was watching through a screen as the bodies became chess pieces that moved this way and that way in what almost seemed like a natural motion despite the limited practice of any of the participants. This elbow fit in that spot, but that knee went somewhere else. This person's voice softened when they moaned, but this other person screamed when they were happy the same way another person screamed when someone stepped on their foot in an awkward way. This person was a little embarrassed and shy until things got going and they became a superstar while this other person was ready for anything beforehand and then became increasingly hesitant when things started happening. It was a fascinating study in nuance that captivated me.

CHAPTER 25

The only times I have managed to enjoy the taste of vodka have involved licking or drinking it off of or out of a human body part. I don't know what to do with this information.

***

A decade ago, I had sex with Alice Cooper. Now, don't get too excited, I don't mean the famous Alice Cooper who has been making a living singing to the world for the last few decades. That is not who I slept with, but I would if he ever gave me the chance. No, I slept with a person who had the same name.

The Alice Cooper I slept with was not the famous shock rocker. My Alice was a waitress that lived in a rural part of Georgia. She was a part time waitress and a part time writer, she said. She was a poet interested in capturing, as she put it, "The way nature envelopes the soul in the minute details of the world." I had no clue what that meant then, and I still can't even formulate a good guess, but that was what she said. I think I slept with her partly because that was the way she talked too. I think I also slept with her because I was bored and lonely on my way to Florida with nothing else to do in a – and I mean this as literally as possible because I saw the damn thing on my drive – one horse town. I think I also slept with her because I was already starting to feel the loneliness that would plague me throughout my first year of graduate school. I think I also slept with her to try to get a girl named Nikki who I'll talk about at some point out of my head after meeting her right before I left for Florida. If I'm being completely honest with you, however, I mainly slept with her so I could say I slept with Alice Cooper and watch the reactions on people's faces before I clarified the statement a few minutes later.

***

I followed in my biological grandfather's footsteps in an unexpected way one weekend when I was in New Orleans. Nikki and I were there to meet up with my birth mom and her sister. Nikki spent most of the time playing video poker in the casino on Canal Street, and my birth mom and I spent most of our time walking around the boardwalk area on the river. It was a peaceful, relatively calm, weekend until we went to a piano bar one night, and Nikki got completely shitfaced. She was utterly hung over and certain she was dying in the hotel room the next afternoon when we woke up so I could say goodbye to my relatives as they left the city. This was how I accidentally followed in my biological grandfather's footsteps.

Nikki was dying and not interested in leaving the bed, much less the hotel room. This was rather understandable considering I had to take special care to get her safely to bed the night before while avoiding the very real possibility that she would fall on her ass. During one of the short periods while she was not sleeping, not vomiting, and not telling me she was dying, she asked me to run down the block and fetch her some food from Krystal's. My biological grandfather was in love with Krystal's, and there are many stories of him eating nothing but these mini fast food creations whenever he visited the area where him and I were raised in different decades. I, on the other hand, had never bothered to even try the damn things. I was hungry too, so I offered to go to three other places that all had something I liked as well. Nikki didn't want any of that, as she called it, "horseshit." She wanted Krystal's. This was how, on a random day in the year 2011, I tried Krystal chicks for the first time in the French Quarter while my spouse was dying in a hotel room a few blocks away.

Like my biological grandfather before me, this moment triggered an insatiable desire for Krystal's at a time when I did not live in an area that had any Krystal's restaurants. I'm not kidding, what are the odds of this type of shit happening, I mean, come on. Well, not surprisingly, I then found myself – as if I was stepping into the past – annoying the shit out of Nikki and everyone else every time we went back to South Carolina to visit family. I did this by camping out at various Krystal's locations to eat those damn tiny chicken sandwiches. I did this for the next few years, long after Nikki and I parted ways actually, but then one day I woke up and simply didn't want them anymore. I remember wondering if my biological grandfather had looked down from some cloud or up from some fire pit and taken pity on me. Maybe, I reasoned, he removed the need so I could visit South Carolina in peace again. I doubt it. Instead, I think the fact that I moved to a city that had more than one Krystal's took all the charm out of my mad dashes to the nearest Krystal's I could find on my trips. Maybe both of these things are true, but maybe neither are. Why do I suddenly want one of those damn tiny chicken sandwiches again?

***

"Are you sure you want to do this," Dexter asked from somewhere behind me. He was 17. I was 15. Gillingham was out of town, and not interested in this type of thing. Kimber was interested in this type of thing. We would try it a few weeks later. Dexter was interested in this type of thing more than anything else. I was curious.

"Yep, do your thing mate," I remember saying right before the whip came crashing into my exposed ass. It was tingly. It hurt a little bit. It was not all that interesting, but it was not bad either. He asked how I was feeling. I said I was fine. He asked if I wanted another. I said why not. He hit me again. I nodded. He hit me again. This went on for a while. It ended when I said it should end. By that point, I was in pain. By that point, my ass was rather sore. By that point, he was breathing heavy. By that point, I was somewhere between bored and still curious. I was bored from the activity. I was curious about the part of the activity I liked a lot. It didn't necessarily make me feel anything when I was being whipped. It was okay, a sometimes food one might say. It did, however, create an incredibly pleasurable set of sensations from my toes to my head to be told what to do, under someone else's control, and yet, safe at the same time. This part, I realized automatically, I really enjoyed. I later learned it was called submission. I later learned I liked it a lot no matter what the activity was or who the person in charge was. I later let him try out a few other things he liked with the promise that he would be in charge, and I would do as I was told. I made the same deal with Kimber.

CHAPTER 25

***

Like many southern parents, mine engaged in what I call psychological warfare when I was a child. Don't get me wrong, they were good Southern Baptists who never spared the rod or spoiled the child. They loved – I felt like it at least – to give a good beating as much as anyone else. At the same time, the more effective mechanisms of control they utilized were mental games that, to me, seemed much crueler and more vicious.

There were the times I was sent out into the front yard to pick the stick that would be used to whoop my ass. This was always a mental challenge. If I picked one that was not hard or big enough, then I knew they would send me back to pick again. I knew this because it happened a couple of times. At the same time, if I picked one too big or too hard, the damn thing might break my back or my ass or the back of my neck or wherever else this whipping might involve before it was over. This was a tricky decision. I had to find the right balance for the weapon that would be used to make me feel horrible. The time between being sent out into the front yard and returning with the weapon of my choice was far worse than even the worst of the beatings. This is what I mean by psychological warfare.

CHAPTER 26

I still see my first love sometimes when I'm walking down this or that street. I know he's not real. I know I'm imagining him or that it's just someone who might look similar in the right light. I know these things, but I still feel myself shake a little bit inside each time I think I see him on this or that street.

***

"Somehow," she said nodding slowly, "We can just spot each other, you know, I mean, I don't know how," she says moving a piece of hair out of her eyes, "I don't know how okay, but those of us who have been hurt, you know, we can somehow just sense others like us, you know." I've been in love – best I can tell, like really in love – three or four times in my life. I've had – best I can tell – three or four other people in my life that I loved in a different, non-romantic, best friend, type of way. I've met many people over the years that I felt close to for one reason or another. Damn near all of these people have experienced some significant trauma related to families, abandonment, violence, or loss. I don't think this is a coincidence.

I began noticing this pattern in the middle of my twenties. There was the realization that each of my five closest friends at the time had all been abused. There was the fourth person I dated in a row who had also been raped – though not necessarily in the same way I was. There was the sixteenth random stranger I had a long conversation with that ultimately resulted in them telling me about some past trauma with the disclaimer that they didn't usually talk about this particular thing. All these things happening at once caught my attention. I noticed that I was somehow surrounded by people dealing with past traumas in numerous ways. This became even more obvious in the one case where I found myself involved – first as casual lovers and later as a couple for a few weeks – with the only person in my life at the time who wasn't dealing with this type of thing. I automatically didn't trust them as much. It felt crazy, but I could not wrap my head around a person without trauma, this made me realize it was everywhere I looked.

After that realization, I began going over the people who had been important to me throughout my life, and I began paying attention to anyone who became close to me. Almost all of them had some traumatic event or multiple events in their lives. It was, and remains, one of the most fascinating things I've noticed. This is because there is no way that I can find – or that any science I've seen can find – to explain it. Somehow, as my friend said so long ago, we seem to be able to see each other, see the pain, see something. I still don't know what it is, but the pattern continues to the present.

***

The other day I was tooling around online when I noticed something especially terrifying. I'm not talking about the latest scandal or crisis. One seems to arise almost every day. I'm not talking about some trend or statistic that some reporter simplified or took out of context to get more clicks. I'm used to that. No, I was terrified by something that is all the more frightening because I seriously doubt, based on a few years as an educator, that most Americans would even realize why I found it alarming. That, I think, is a special kind of fear.

What terrified me was actually a purse. The idea of a purse is not scary to me, but this was a purse that was made through the destruction of a book. Let that sink in for a second. Books, you know, the first thing any fascist regime destroys and takes away, the little things that have led to all out wars over the simple right to own and be able to read one of them, and the things that people died to be allowed to have, read, and share with others, yeah, books. It was one of those all too common videos about arts and crafts where someone with too much time on their hands shows you a new way to make something that is supposedly trendy. In this case, the new way to make a nice purse was to take a book, rip out the words and pages of the book, and then bind it back together as a purse. If this doesn't frighten you, then you are probably one of the many Americans who have no clue how things have gotten so bad in our country. Reading is almost always part of such down swings in nations. We don't read. We don't care about reading. Fascists don't need to burn our books because we will destroy them ourselves in the name of fashion without any coercion necessary. That, my friend, is horrifying.

***

One of the things I hated most as a child was fishing. It was boring. It was disgusting. It was hot. There was never any music on the boat because my dad was there. I couldn't read because my parents were both there. It was terrible. Well, it was terrible until I figured out how to annoy my parents just enough to not have to go anymore, but not enough to get my ass whipped.

We would go out to the lake an hour or two, I can't remember, from where we lived, and my parents would take this incredibly old – and to my eyes, way too nasty – yellow boat out on the lake. This part was fun. We would cruise over the waves, and I would enjoy the splashing sounds. Then, unfortunately, we would slow to a crawl or even sit still for hours in some cove or bay or whatever where there was nothing, no one, and silence. It was so quiet. Since my parents rarely say much of anything, this was almost the perfect recipe for boredom. When I was nine, however, I realized that if I started talking at random intervals and singing from time to time, it would drive them – read, my dad – crazy. He would start yelling about me scaring the fish, and we would be in each of the coves and out on the lake overall a much shorter time. When I realized this, I started doing it all the time, and it only took six more trips after that point before I never had to go fishing again.

***

There are certain childhood experiences that stick with you for no goddamn reason. Maybe it is the street you played on that one time with that one new toy you didn't like all that much. Maybe it is that neighbor who never seemed all that important until they moved away. Maybe it is some song that annoys the shit out of you even though you sing along when it comes on the radio. Maybe, as in my case, it is the time the little boy started swinging his penis in the front yard of your neighbor's house for everyone to see.

I really have no clue why I remember this day, but it stuck with me. The little boy was a friend of mine's youngest brother. The other brother was a little bit nuts too, I admit. I say this after noting the penis waving youngest, and I know that seems odd, but here me out. The middle brother would get upset and do all kinds of crazy shit. There was this one day when he wanted to borrow a CD from his neighbor, but she said no. He proceeded to walk into his backyard, beat himself up leaving bruises on his face and blood coming from his nose, and then go inside and tell his mother that the neighbor stole his CD and beat him up. She didn't believe him for a second, but that much effort, even in a loss, was just kind of wild and also normal for him. In any case, he was nuts, but the youngest brother was just a bit of an exhibitionist.

There was the time he came outside and just started randomly swinging his penis and laughing at the group of us older kids standing nearby. There was the time he sat for about an hour, we counted if you're curious, in the bay window of his house with his ass pressed against the glass. That took patience. There was the time he squatted and took a shit in the middle of the street while the mail carrier was filling his family's box. This was all before he even got to the age of 8, and it only got worse. He was arrested six times in high school for flashing this or that person – usually old people for some reason – and at one point he made a video of himself masturbating that he distributed via locker to half the kids in his class. I never can figure out why I even remember this kid since I barely spoke nine words to him in the few years he lived on my block, but I guess there is something about a tiny swinging dick that sticks in your head.

CHAPTER 27

Sometimes people call me doctor. Sometimes they call me mam. Sometimes they call me sir. Sometimes I wonder if I'll ever have any clue who I am. Sometimes I wonder if that even really matters after all this time.

***

My other counselor, the one that said I talked too much when we were in bed together, said I was probably a sociopath. When I first heard this term, I had an image of Hannibal Lecter or some other serial killer. She pointed out that those were examples, but that other examples were great prophets, teachers, and artists throughout history. She said it depended on what you did with the ability to live beyond norms and rules; what your own self-created moral system included. A villain would use such a thing to take over or control others. A hero would use such a thing to inspire and help others. I think I unconsciously became a little of both.

Now, don't get me wrong here doc, I'm not trying to put myself down or raise myself up by saying this, I don't even know if I agree with her, you know? It's just, well, it's our first meeting after the nine times I came here, smoked cigarettes, and didn't come in, and well, I felt like this would be a good introduction because you're right, I don't know what the hell I'm going to say here, I mean, I get it, I was raised in the south so some things like Baptists, the Civil War, time spent in fields or with scarecrows or fishing or whatever, I get it, some things I guess I have to talk about for you to have any idea, you know, but I don't know what I'm going to say, and I'm still not sure how I feel about being recorded, you know, but I guess that gives me a start, you know, that was the last time, well the only time really, that I really tried to talk to someone, you know, to try to figure out this shit, I guess me, I'm this shit, right, but yeah, to figure me out and I guess this seems like a place to start, you know?

**

The most important part of getting ready for a next step or life change, for me, is to listen to my entire record collection – whatever style or shape it is in – before the step or change. After college, I did this before selling most and getting the rest unexpectedly destroyed. After deciding to go to college, same thing. After graduate school, same thing but all I had were digital albums at that point and one Americana CD that I got cheap. It's a ritual that calms me, I guess, and I do it every time something massive is shifting.

While I've been going through these latest self-discovery attempts and getting ready to either move to another part of the planet or off the planet entirely, whatever I decide, I've been pleased at the size of my vinyl and CD collection in the few years since graduate school. I've been listening to CD's in no particular order in the car, and then listening to my records – starting with Z and going all the way to the last one where the artist's name starts with a number today – as the lease runs out. I might go east this time for a new adventure with my boxed-up records and CD's. I might go away altogether this time. I might stay here but move to another neighborhood. I've never been good at staying in the same place or the same home for very long, so I know I have to leave, but as usual, I don't know why. Luckily, the only things I really own that I would be upset to lose again are my records and CD's – they don't complain much or seem to care where I live. The wine tingles on my lips as I sit on my porch staring into the courtyard and listening to the silence that remains when the record finishes. That silence, for me, says more than most words probably could.

**

Though I have a couple recurring nightmares from when I was a child that I will probably mention at some point even though I doubt I'll talk about them in depth, there is one that arose in my twenties as well. This one, at times even more so than the ones from childhood, bothers me on many levels, but also makes more sense to me than the others without much thought or reflection. I never know when it will return, but each time, I know it will return.

I am standing in the field near my house as a child. If I haven't mentioned the field yet, I will a lot I'm sure. Anyhow, there was a scarecrow in the field that I would go talk to when I was young, and I even took its place once to scare children, but that's another story. Anyway, in the dream I am out in the field talking to the scarecrow when, without any warning, I become the scarecrow and I am locked into the pole somehow. I cannot move. I dream about this field a lot so this opening to the nightmare is even more terrible because it is always a surprise. I realize I'm in the nightmare when I become the scarecrow and cannot move. It is even more odd because sometimes, in this dream only, I know I'm in a dream even while it is happening, and yet somehow, that doesn't make it any less frightening or difficult. I am there, locked into the pole, stuck in the moment, and then the terrifying part begins.

It is always the same. It has never changed in form, though more people have been added over the years, which, I guess, is only natural. The scarecrow from the field sat in the midst of a crop of corn the whole time I was a child. From the corn, one-by-one, people come into the little clearing where the scarecrow stood, where I am stuck in place with no ability to move or speak. Did I mention I can't speak in the dream? I can't. I don't know if it would be less terrible if I could, but I do wonder about that. Anyhow, people begin coming into the clearing. They come one at a time until the end of the dream where, in a split second, the clearing fills up with all them saying the same thing in unison. This happens later. First, they come alone.

Sometimes all of them come by the end of the dream, but at other times, only a portion of them come to talk to me individually. They are always all there at the end when they speak in unison. Gillingham always comes. My grandmother who was biologically my great-grandmother always comes. My oldest sister always comes. Since 2014, my birth mother always comes. The others are more random. Some of them come a lot. Some of them have only come for an one conversation – well, speech, I guess, since I can't respond. The individual sessions always include more than just the three – and since 2014, the four – that always come. The lowest amount of individual sessions so far has been 7. I don't know if this is significant. It is just what has happened so far.

The individual sessions are always the same. They begin by noting something I have done in the years since that particular person died. It may be something good, but it is usually something most people would not think is good based on the morals of our time. More importantly, even when it is something that might be good, it is always something that I know that particular person would not like or consider good in their own life. After this introduction, they ask me how I am doing as if I could respond – I always wonder if they know I cannot talk. Next, they always ask why I continue to live when they had to die. They always say they had to die. They often suggest it was at least somehow my fault or that it was so I could continue to live. I wonder if these are emotions I feel that I do not know how to access consciously. Finally, they always tell me about some amazing thing they would have done – and they know they would have done it now that they can see beyond my mortal vision – if they had lived instead of me. These things they would have definitely done that would have definitely done more good than I do take a wide variety of forms that I won't go into here.

The nightmare always ends the same way. There is never any variation in it at all, aside from adding more people since I first had this dream at the age of 24. The individuals – both those who came by for one talk and the others – all show up in the clearing at the same time. I don't see them enter they are just there. In the same voice, kind of like they are all shouting in unison, but also kind of like they share one voice now, they always say the same thing. They repeat it at least 39 times so far in every dream, but sometimes a couple more, maybe for good measure, I don't know. They say, "I'm dead, why did you live?" They say it again, and for the first time, I'm glad I can't talk because I don't know. They keep saying it, and then, at some point, I wake up. I wake up, but I can still hear them.

CHAPTER 28

39 hours shy of 34 days of nightmares and too many suicidal impulses led me to the office of a counselor I found online on my 35th birthday...

SUGGESTED CLASS ROOM OR BOOK CLUB USE

DISCUSSION QUESTIONS

1. *Scarecrow* explores the complexities of the life course. What are some ways your own experience of life has shifted and changed over time?
2. Throughout the novel, Erin seeks to figure out who she is and how she got to her current life. What are some things that tell you who you are? How did you get to this point in your life?
3. *Scarecrow* focuses heavily on life in the southeastern United States. What are some ways your own impressions of the south mirror or depart from Erin's experiences?
4. Erin forms and maintains varied types of relationships throughout the book. Think of your own life and relationships, how do these experiences compare?
5. The novel explores some ways race, class, gender, and sexualities may shape the experiences of people in society. What are some ways, positive and/or negative, that race, class, gender, and sexualities may shape your own life, relationships, and experiences?

CREATIVE WRITING ASSIGNMENTS

1. Pick one of Erin's experiences you can relate to, and think about it. Compose a story about how you relate to that experience.
2. Re-write the first chapter of the novel from the perspective of another person who differs in some way socially from Erin.
3. Pick a place in the life course, and write a story about how Erin might experience that point of her life.
4. Beginning after the final chapter of the novel, continue Erin's narration, what happens to her after counseling?

QUALITATIVE RESEARCH ACTIVITIES

1. Select any conversation or event in the book and conduct a focus group to learn how other people interpret that conversation or event.
2. Erin talks about varied norms in the south including but not limited to how people talk or deal with new information. Conduct an interview study to see how people in your own social world narrate some kind of norm or meaning that is important to them.

ABOUT THE AUTHOR

J.E. Sumerau is the author of five novels – *Cigarettes & Wine*, *Homecoming Queens*, *Other People's Oysters* (with Alexandra C.H. Nowakowski), *Palmetto Rose*, and *Via Chicago* – as well as two novellas, *Essence* and *That Year*, and over 80 scholarly works concerning the intersections of sexualities, gender, health, religion, and violence in society. She is also an associate professor and the director of applied sociology at the University of Tampa as well as the co-founder and primary editor of www.writewhereithurts.net. For more information, please visit www.jsumerau.com or follow her on Twitter @jsumerau.

Printed in the United States
by Baker & Taylor Publisher Services